Cloud Storage Made Simple
Your Guide to

Dropbox

Kiet Huynh

Table of Contents

Introduction 6
   1.1 What is Dropbox? 6
   1.2 Why Use Cloud Storage? 10
   1.3 How This Book Will Help You 14

CHAPTER I Getting Started with Dropbox 18
   1.1 Setting Up Your Account 18
      1.1.1 Creating a Free Account 18
      1.1.2 Choosing the Right Plan 22
      1.1.3 Understanding Storage Limits 26
   1.2 Installing Dropbox on Your Devices 31
      1.2.1 Desktop Installation 31
      1.2.2 Mobile App Installation 35
      1.2.3 Configuring Sync Settings 39
   1.3 Navigating the Interface 45
      1.3.1 Desktop Interface Overview 45
      1.3.2 Mobile App Navigation 52
      1.3.3 Key Features in the Web Version 56

CHAPTER II Uploading and Organizing Files 63
   2.1 Uploading Files to Dropbox 63
      2.1.1 Drag-and-Drop Uploads 63
      2.1.2 Uploading via Mobile App 68
      2.1.3 Using the File Request Feature 72
   2.2 Creating and Managing Folders 78
      2.2.1 Best Practices for Folder Organization 78
      2.2.2 Renaming and Moving Files 82

TABLE OF CONTENTS

    2.2.3 Deleting and Recovering Files 86
  2.3 Searching for Files 92
    2.3.1 Using the Search Bar 92
    2.3.2 Filtering Results 95
    2.3.3 Recent and Starred Files 100
CHAPTER III Sharing and Collaboration **105**
  3.1 Sharing Files and Folders 105
    3.1.1 Sharing Links 105
    3.1.2 Setting Permissions for Shared Files 110
    3.1.3 Managing Shared Folders 114
  3.2 Collaborating with Others 119
    3.2.1 Real-Time Editing with Dropbox Paper 119
    3.2.2 Commenting on Files 123
    3.2.3 Activity Notifications and Logs 128
  3.3 Dropbox for Teams 133
    3.3.1 Setting Up a Team Account 133
    3.3.2 Managing Team Members and Roles 138
    3.3.3 Collaborative Tools for Teams 142
CHAPTER IV Advanced Features and Integrations **148**
  4.1 Version History and File Recovery 148
    4.1.1 Viewing Version History 148
    4.1.2 Restoring Previous Versions 153
    4.1.3 Managing Deleted Files 158
  4.2 Offline Access 163
    4.2.1 Setting Up Offline Files 163
    4.2.2 Managing Offline Preferences 167
    4.2.3 Troubleshooting Offline Sync Issues 170
  4.3 Integrating Dropbox with Other Tools 176

TABLE OF CONTENTS

    4.3.1 Integrations with Google Workspace 176

    4.3.2 Using Dropbox with Microsoft Office 180

    4.3.3 Connecting Dropbox to Slack and Trello 184

CHAPTER V Security and Privacy **189**

  5.1 Securing Your Account 189

    5.1.1 Enabling Two-Factor Authentication 189

    5.1.2 Setting Strong Passwords 192

    5.1.3 Recognizing Suspicious Activity 196

  5.2 Managing Permissions and Access 200

    5.2.1 Sharing with Limited Access 200

    5.2.2 Revoking Access from Users 203

    5.2.3 Adjusting Team Permissions 208

  5.3 Data Privacy 213

    5.3.1 Understanding Dropbox's Privacy Policy 213

    5.3.2 Tips for Protecting Your Data 217

    5.3.3 Handling Compliance Requirements 221

CHAPTER VI Troubleshooting and FAQs **226**

  6.1 Common Issues and Solutions 226

    6.1.1 Sync Problems 226

    6.1.2 Login Issues 230

    6.1.3 File Upload Errors 235

  6.2 Getting Help 239

    6.2.1 Using the Help Center 239

    6.2.2 Contacting Dropbox Support 243

    6.2.3 Community Forums and Tips 248

  6.3 Staying Updated 252

    6.3.1 New Features and Announcements 252

    6.3.2 Beta Testing Dropbox Features 257

TABLE OF CONTENTS

    6.3.3 Keeping Your Apps Up-to-Date 261

Conclusion 266

7.1 Recap of Key Features 266

7.2 Tips for Maximizing Dropbox 271

7.3 Final Thoughts on Cloud Storage 276

Acknowledgments 280

Introduction

1.1 What is Dropbox?

Dropbox is a cloud storage platform that allows individuals and businesses to store, share, and access files from virtually anywhere. Founded in 2007, Dropbox has become a pioneer in the field of cloud storage, offering users a seamless and efficient way to manage digital files without being tied to a specific device. But what exactly is Dropbox, and why has it become a cornerstone for millions of users worldwide? This section will delve into the key features, functionalities, and benefits of Dropbox to give you a comprehensive understanding of its role in modern file management.

A Cloud-Based Storage Solution

At its core, Dropbox is a service that lets you save files in the cloud. Instead of keeping all your files on your local computer or external hard drives, Dropbox stores them securely on remote servers. This means your data is not only safe from physical damage, such as hardware failure or accidental deletion, but also accessible anytime, anywhere, with an internet connection.

Cloud storage offers significant advantages:

- **Accessibility**: Whether you're on your desktop at home, using your smartphone on the go, or logging in from a borrowed laptop, you can access your files instantly.

- **Space Efficiency**: Instead of consuming storage space on your device, Dropbox frees up local memory by offloading large files to the cloud.

The Origins of Dropbox

Dropbox was founded by Drew Houston and Arash Ferdowsi, who identified a common frustration: the inability to access important files across multiple devices easily. They envisioned a platform where files could sync automatically, and Dropbox was born. Over the years, Dropbox has evolved from a simple file-syncing tool to a comprehensive collaboration and productivity suite.

How Dropbox Works

Dropbox operates on a straightforward principle: sync, store, and share.

1. **Sync**: Dropbox synchronizes files across devices. When you upload a file to Dropbox on one device, it becomes available on all linked devices.
2. **Store**: Files are securely stored on Dropbox's servers, which use advanced encryption to ensure data safety.
3. **Share**: Sharing files and folders with others is as simple as generating a link. Permissions can be adjusted to control access levels.

Features of Dropbox

Dropbox provides an array of features designed to make file management efficient and intuitive:

1. **File Syncing**
    - Dropbox ensures that any changes made to a file are reflected across all devices in real time. This eliminates versioning conflicts and ensures consistency.

2. **File Sharing**
    - Whether you're sharing a single document or an entire folder, Dropbox makes collaboration easy. You can grant view-only access or editing rights and even password-protect shared files.

3. **Collaboration Tools**
    - Dropbox Paper is an integrated tool for team collaboration, enabling users to create, edit, and comment on documents in real time.

4. **Offline Access**

- Files can be made available offline, allowing you to work without an internet connection. Changes are synced once you reconnect.

5. **Version History and Recovery**
   - Dropbox keeps a history of file changes, making it possible to recover earlier versions or deleted files for up to 30 days (or longer for premium users).

6. **Third-Party Integrations**
   - Dropbox integrates seamlessly with tools like Google Workspace, Microsoft Office, and Slack, enhancing productivity across platforms.

Who Uses Dropbox?

Dropbox caters to a broad audience, including:

- **Individuals**: For personal use, Dropbox is ideal for backing up important documents, photos, and videos.
- **Small Businesses**: Teams can use Dropbox to collaborate on projects, share resources, and maintain a centralized file repository.
- **Enterprises**: With advanced security features and team management tools, Dropbox is suitable for larger organizations that need secure and scalable cloud solutions.

Advantages of Dropbox

Dropbox's popularity stems from several key benefits:

1. **Ease of Use**
   - The intuitive interface ensures that even beginners can start using Dropbox without a steep learning curve.

2. **Cross-Platform Compatibility**
   - Dropbox works across various operating systems, including Windows, macOS, iOS, and Android, ensuring seamless access regardless of the device.

3. **Reliable Security**

- Dropbox employs industry-standard encryption to protect your data during transfer and storage. Additionally, features like two-factor authentication add an extra layer of security.

4. **Scalability**
    - Whether you need a basic plan for personal use or an advanced enterprise plan for your organization, Dropbox offers a range of options.

Limitations of Dropbox

While Dropbox is a powerful tool, it's not without limitations:

1. **Storage Costs**
    - Free accounts are limited to 2GB, which may not suffice for users with large storage needs. Paid plans offer more space but may be costly for some.

2. **Dependence on Internet**
    - A stable internet connection is essential for syncing and accessing files stored in the cloud.

Conclusion

Dropbox has transformed the way people manage and share files, offering a blend of convenience, security, and collaboration. Whether you're an individual looking to back up precious memories, a professional needing to access work documents on the go, or a team aiming to streamline collaboration, Dropbox provides a versatile solution. As you progress through this guide, you'll gain a deeper understanding of how to leverage Dropbox's features to simplify and enhance your digital life.

1.2 Why Use Cloud Storage?

In an age dominated by digital data, cloud storage has emerged as one of the most indispensable tools for individuals and organizations. Whether you're a student managing academic projects, a professional working on collaborative tasks, or a business owner safeguarding critical data, cloud storage offers a plethora of advantages that traditional storage methods cannot rival. This section delves into the key reasons why cloud storage, particularly Dropbox, has become a cornerstone of modern data management.

Easy Accessibility Anytime, Anywhere

One of the most compelling reasons to use cloud storage is its unparalleled accessibility. Unlike physical storage devices, which are location-dependent, cloud storage allows you to access your files from virtually anywhere in the world. With Dropbox, all you need is an internet connection and a compatible device—be it a computer, smartphone, or tablet—to access your data instantly.

Imagine being on a business trip and needing an important document stored on your office computer. With Dropbox, such concerns become a thing of the past. Simply log into your account, and the document is at your fingertips. This convenience is particularly valuable in today's hybrid work environments, where professionals often switch between home and office setups.

Seamless Collaboration

Collaboration is at the heart of many projects, and cloud storage platforms like Dropbox excel in this area. Traditional methods of sharing files—such as email attachments—can be cumbersome and inefficient, especially when multiple people need to access and edit the same document. Dropbox simplifies collaboration by enabling real-time sharing and editing.

For example, Dropbox Paper, a built-in feature, allows team members to work on the same document simultaneously, with changes synced in real time. Team members can leave comments, assign tasks, and track progress—all within the platform. This level of integration ensures that everyone stays on the same page, enhancing productivity and reducing miscommunication.

Enhanced Security

Data security is a top priority in an era where cyber threats are increasingly sophisticated. Many users might hesitate to trust cloud storage because of security concerns, but Dropbox has implemented robust measures to safeguard your data.

Dropbox employs advanced encryption protocols to protect your files during transfer and storage. Additionally, features like two-factor authentication (2FA) add an extra layer of security, ensuring that only authorized users can access your account. For businesses, Dropbox offers enterprise-level security options, including advanced permissions management and detailed activity logs, to monitor and control data access.

Automatic Backups

Data loss is a nightmare scenario for anyone, whether due to accidental deletion, hardware failure, or cyberattacks. Cloud storage serves as a reliable backup solution, automatically syncing your files and ensuring they're always up to date.

With Dropbox, you can set your files to sync automatically across all connected devices. This means that even if your primary device is lost, damaged, or stolen, your files remain safe in the cloud. Additionally, Dropbox offers file version history, allowing you to restore previous versions of your files if needed—ideal for recovering from mistakes or overwriting errors.

Cost-Effective Scalability

Traditional storage solutions often require significant upfront investments in hardware, not to mention the costs of maintenance and upgrades. In contrast, cloud storage is highly scalable and cost-effective, making it suitable for users with varying needs.

Dropbox offers multiple plans, from free options with basic storage to premium subscriptions for individuals and businesses. This flexibility ensures that you only pay for what you need. Moreover, as your storage requirements grow, upgrading your plan is a seamless process, eliminating the need for physical upgrades or replacements.

Streamlined File Organization

Organizing files effectively can be a daunting task, especially when dealing with large amounts of data. Dropbox simplifies this process with intuitive features that help you categorize, search, and manage files effortlessly.

The platform allows you to create folders, apply tags, and mark files as starred for easy access. Its powerful search functionality can locate files based on names, keywords, or even content, saving you time and effort. Additionally, Dropbox's Smart Sync feature enables you to manage storage space by keeping less frequently used files online while still appearing in your local file directory.

Environmental Benefits

Switching to cloud storage can also have a positive environmental impact. By reducing reliance on physical storage devices and paper-based file management, cloud storage contributes to a decrease in electronic waste and deforestation.

Dropbox data centers are optimized for energy efficiency, and the company has committed to sustainability initiatives. For environmentally conscious users and businesses, adopting cloud storage is a step toward reducing their carbon footprint while enjoying advanced technological benefits.

Flexibility Across Devices and Platforms

Dropbox is designed to work seamlessly across various devices and operating systems, including Windows, macOS, Android, and iOS. This cross-platform compatibility ensures that you can switch between devices without any disruption to your workflow.

For example, you can start editing a document on your desktop, continue working on it using your tablet during a commute, and make final adjustments on your smartphone. Dropbox's synchronization capabilities ensure that all changes are instantly updated across devices, providing a seamless user experience.

Disaster Recovery

Natural disasters, hardware malfunctions, and cyberattacks can result in catastrophic data loss for individuals and organizations. Cloud storage serves as a reliable disaster recovery solution, ensuring that your critical data remains secure even in worst-case scenarios.

Dropbox maintains multiple copies of your files across its global network of servers, providing redundancy that minimizes the risk of data loss. This ensures that even if a server experiences issues, your files remain accessible.

Future-Proofing Your Data Management

As technology evolves, the ways we manage and store data will continue to change. By adopting cloud storage, you're investing in a solution that keeps pace with technological advancements. Dropbox regularly updates its features, incorporating user feedback and innovations to meet modern needs.

From integrating with emerging tools like AI-powered assistants to supporting advanced collaboration features, Dropbox ensures that you're always equipped with cutting-edge capabilities for managing your data.

Conclusion

Cloud storage is more than just a convenient way to store files—it's a transformative tool that enhances accessibility, collaboration, security, and efficiency. Dropbox stands out as a leading provider in this space, offering user-friendly features and robust security measures to meet the demands of modern life. Whether you're an individual, a team, or a business, adopting cloud storage like Dropbox is an investment in productivity and peace of mind.

1.3 How This Book Will Help You

The world of cloud storage can sometimes feel overwhelming, especially for beginners. Dropbox is a powerful tool with countless features designed to make your personal and professional life more organized and efficient. However, unlocking its full potential requires a clear understanding of its capabilities and best practices. This book is your roadmap, providing step-by-step guidance to help you master Dropbox from the ground up.

Comprehensive Guidance for All Skill Levels

Whether you're new to Dropbox or already have some experience with cloud storage, this book is designed to cater to all users. If you're just starting out, the beginner-friendly approach will walk you through the basics, such as creating an account, uploading files, and navigating the interface. For more advanced users, detailed explanations of Dropbox's collaboration tools, integrations, and security settings will deepen your expertise.

For businesses and teams, the book includes a dedicated chapter on how Dropbox can enhance workplace collaboration and streamline project management. By the time you finish reading, you'll feel confident using Dropbox to meet your personal and professional needs.

Clear, Step-by-Step Instructions

Complex technical guides can be intimidating. This book simplifies the learning process by breaking down each feature into easy-to-follow steps. Each chapter includes:

- **Detailed walkthroughs**: Screenshots and step-by-step instructions to help you complete tasks without confusion.

- **Practical examples**: Real-world scenarios demonstrating how Dropbox can be applied in everyday life.

- **Pro tips**: Advanced techniques and shortcuts to save you time and effort.

From uploading your first file to managing team accounts, every feature is explained in a way that feels approachable and manageable.

Practical Use Cases

One of the unique aspects of this book is its emphasis on practical application. Instead of simply explaining how Dropbox works, it shows you why and when you should use certain features. Whether you're organizing your personal photos, collaborating on a group project, or backing up important business documents, this book provides scenarios that mirror real-life challenges.

Here are some examples of use cases covered in this book:

- **For individuals**: Learn how to store and organize your family photos, access files on the go, and share important documents securely.
- **For students**: Discover how Dropbox can help you manage coursework, collaborate on group assignments, and keep track of academic materials.
- **For small businesses**: Master file-sharing with clients, collaborate efficiently with your team, and streamline document management.

Insights into Advanced Features

While Dropbox is user-friendly, some of its most powerful features often go unnoticed. This book explores advanced capabilities such as:

- **Version history**: Recover previous versions of files to safeguard against mistakes.
- **Smart Sync**: Save space on your computer by keeping files online but easily accessible.
- **Dropbox integrations**: Connect Dropbox with tools like Google Workspace, Microsoft Office, and Slack to streamline your workflow.

These advanced features can significantly enhance productivity and security, and this book ensures you know how to use them effectively.

Focus on Security and Privacy

In an era where data security is a top concern, this book dedicates a full chapter to Dropbox's robust security features. You'll learn how to:

- Set up two-factor authentication for extra protection.
- Manage file-sharing permissions to control access.
- Understand Dropbox's privacy policies and compliance with regulations.

By following these steps, you can use Dropbox with confidence, knowing that your files are secure.

Optimized for Productivity

Time is precious, and this book is designed to help you get the most out of Dropbox without wasting a moment. You'll find tips and strategies for:

- **Streamlining your workflow**: Organize files efficiently and keep your folders clutter-free.
- **Collaborating effortlessly**: Share files with teammates and track their updates in real-time.
- **Automating repetitive tasks**: Use integrations and shortcuts to save time on routine actions.

Empowering Teams and Organizations

Dropbox isn't just for individual use—it's also a powerful tool for teams. This book includes a dedicated section on team collaboration, covering topics like:

- Setting up a Dropbox Business account for your organization.
- Using shared folders and team spaces to centralize projects.
- Managing roles and permissions to ensure seamless teamwork.

Whether you're part of a small team or a larger organization, this book will show you how Dropbox can foster communication, productivity, and transparency.

Continuous Learning and Updates

Technology evolves rapidly, and Dropbox is no exception. This book equips you with the skills and mindset to stay updated on new features and improvements. You'll learn how to:

- Access Dropbox's Help Center for ongoing support.
- Join beta programs to test upcoming features.
- Adapt to updates and leverage new capabilities effectively.

Accessible Anytime, Anywhere

The greatest advantage of Dropbox is its ability to provide access to your files no matter where you are. With the skills you gain from this book, you'll have the confidence to:

- Work remotely without interruptions.
- Quickly retrieve critical files during meetings or trips.
- Share resources instantly, improving communication and collaboration.

A Tool for Every Aspect of Your Life

This book isn't just about teaching you how to use Dropbox; it's about empowering you to make the most of cloud storage in every facet of your life. By the end of this guide, you'll have the knowledge and tools to stay organized, improve productivity, and simplify the way you manage digital files.

Take the first step towards mastering Dropbox and transforming your digital organization today. This book is here to support you every step of the way.

CHAPTER I
Getting Started with Dropbox

1.1 Setting Up Your Account

1.1.1 Creating a Free Account

Dropbox offers a simple and intuitive process to create a free account, allowing users to get started with cloud storage quickly. A free account provides 2 GB of storage space and access to core features, making it an ideal starting point for personal use or exploring Dropbox's capabilities. Below, we'll guide you through the process of setting up your account, step-by-step, ensuring that you can start using Dropbox with ease.

Step 1: Visit the Dropbox Website or Download the App

To begin, you'll need to navigate to the official Dropbox website (www.dropbox.com) or download the Dropbox app from your device's app store. Both the desktop and mobile versions allow you to create an account, so choose the option that suits your preference.

Desktop Setup:

- Open your web browser and type in the Dropbox URL.
- Click the "Sign Up" button located in the top-right corner of the homepage.

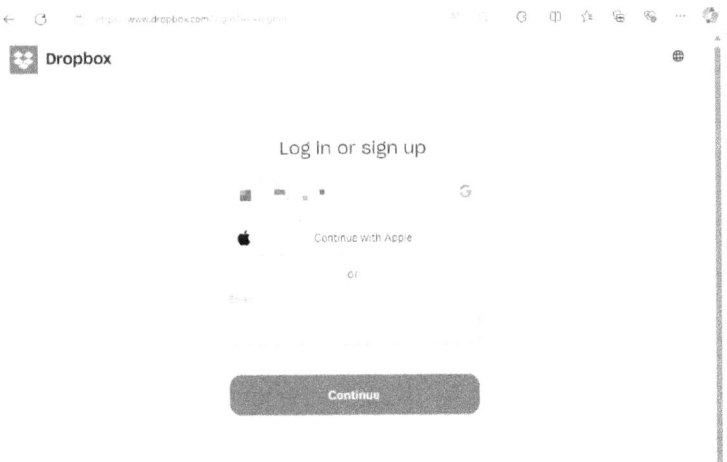

Mobile Setup:

- Search for "Dropbox" in your device's app store (Google Play for Android or App Store for iOS).

- Download and install the app. Once installed, open the app and select "Sign Up."

Step 2: Provide Your Personal Information

Dropbox requires minimal personal information to create an account. On the sign-up page, you'll be asked to provide:

- **Your Full Name**: Enter your first and last name. This will help identify your account, especially when sharing files with others.

- **Email Address**: Use a valid email address you have access to, as it will be used for account verification and recovery.

- **Password**: Create a strong password that includes a mix of letters, numbers, and symbols for added security.

Ensure that the details you provide are accurate, as they will be crucial for accessing your account and troubleshooting any issues in the future.

Step 3: Agree to the Terms of Service

Before proceeding, you'll need to accept Dropbox's terms of service and privacy policy. It's a good practice to review these documents to understand how your data will be handled and what you can expect from the service.

- Check the box to indicate your agreement.
- Optionally, you can choose whether to receive promotional emails from Dropbox.

Step 4: Verify Your Email Address

After completing the sign-up form, Dropbox will send a verification email to the address you provided. Follow these steps to verify your account:

1. Open your email inbox and look for a message from Dropbox.
2. Click the verification link in the email. This action confirms that you own the email address and activates your account.
3. If you don't see the email, check your spam or junk folder, or request a new verification email.

Step 5: Set Up Your Account Preferences

Once your account is activated, Dropbox will prompt you to customize your experience. You may be asked to:

- Choose your preferred language.
- Enable notifications for updates and sharing activities.
- Opt into Dropbox's introductory tutorial, which provides a quick overview of its key features.

Exploring the Free Plan Benefits

As a free account user, you'll have access to essential features, including:

- **2 GB of Storage**: Perfect for storing personal files, photos, and small projects.

- **File Syncing Across Devices**: Keep your files updated and accessible from anywhere.

- **Basic Sharing Options**: Share links to files and folders with friends, family, or colleagues.

- **Dropbox Basic Apps**: Use the desktop, mobile, and web applications to manage your files efficiently.

While the free plan offers limited storage, it's an excellent way to familiarize yourself with Dropbox's capabilities before considering an upgrade.

Tips for a Smooth Setup Process

- **Double-Check Your Email**: Ensure you use a valid email address and verify it promptly.

- **Secure Your Password**: Avoid using common passwords and consider using a password manager for added security.

- **Update Your Profile**: Add a profile picture and update your name if necessary to make your account easily identifiable during collaborations.

Troubleshooting Common Issues

If you encounter any problems while creating your account, here are some common solutions:

- **Issue: Verification Email Not Received**
    - Check your spam or junk folder.
    - Ensure the email address you entered is correct.
    - Request a new verification email via the Dropbox website.

- **Issue: Password Not Accepted**
    - Ensure your password meets Dropbox's complexity requirements.
    - Avoid using previously used passwords if you've had a Dropbox account before.

- **Issue: Unable to Access the Website or App**
    - Check your internet connection.
    - Ensure you're using the latest version of your browser or the app.

Moving Forward

With your account successfully created, you're ready to explore Dropbox's interface and features. Whether you're using it for personal storage or professional collaboration, the free account serves as a robust starting point. In the next section, we'll guide you through installing Dropbox on your devices, ensuring seamless access to your files anytime, anywhere.

1.1.2 Choosing the Right Plan

Selecting the right Dropbox plan is an essential step in optimizing your experience with the platform. Dropbox offers a variety of plans tailored to different needs, whether you're an individual user, a small business owner, or part of a larger organization. In this section, we'll break down the available options, discuss key features, and guide you in selecting the plan that best suits your needs.

Understanding Dropbox Plan Categories

Dropbox divides its offerings into three main categories:

- **Free Plan (Dropbox Basic):** Ideal for personal use and light file storage.
- **Individual Plans:** These include the Plus and Family plans, which are better suited for users who require more storage and additional features.
- **Team and Business Plans:** Designed for professional teams and organizations, offering advanced tools for collaboration and security.

CHAPTER 1: GETTING STARTED WITH DROPBOX

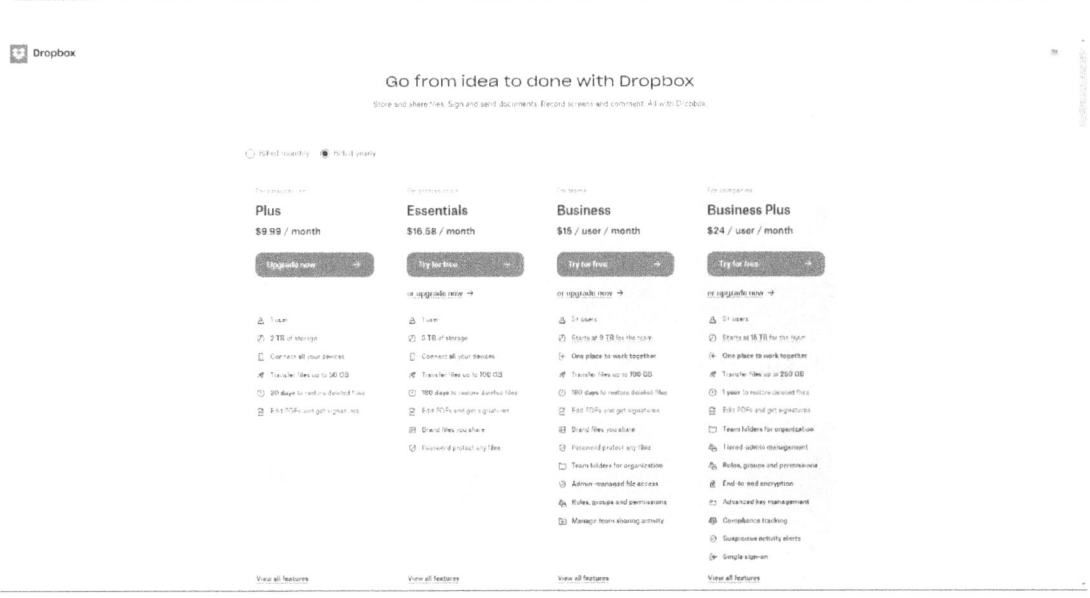

Let's explore these options in detail.

Dropbox Basic: The Free Plan

The Dropbox Basic plan is a great starting point for first-time users. It provides 2 GB of storage space at no cost and is sufficient for lightweight users who need to store documents, photos, and small media files.

Key Features of Dropbox Basic:

- 2 GB of cloud storage.
- Access to Dropbox across multiple devices.
- File sharing with basic permissions.
- Access to Dropbox Paper for real-time collaboration.

Is Dropbox Basic Right for You?

If you're just starting with cloud storage and don't have large storage needs, the Basic plan can be an excellent way to explore Dropbox without any financial commitment. However, it might not be sufficient for users dealing with high-resolution media, large file backups, or extensive collaboration.

Individual Plans: Dropbox Plus and Family

If you find yourself quickly running out of storage on the Basic plan, or if you want additional features like advanced sharing controls and offline access, consider upgrading to an Individual plan.

1. Dropbox Plus

- **Storage:** 2 TB (2,000 GB) of space, ample for most individual users.
- **Offline Access:** Save files locally on your devices to access them without an internet connection.
- **Smart Sync:** Automatically free up space on your computer by storing less frequently used files in the cloud.
- **Advanced Sharing Options:** Password-protected and expiring links for secure file sharing.

Who Should Choose Dropbox Plus?

This plan is perfect for professionals, students, and hobbyists who need a reliable platform for storing and sharing large amounts of data. For example, photographers and videographers often rely on the Plus plan to manage their media libraries.

2. Dropbox Family

- **Storage:** Shared 2 TB of storage for up to six members.
- **Centralized Billing:** One billing account for the entire family.
- **Individual Accounts:** Each family member gets their own Dropbox account with personalized settings.
- **Parental Controls:** Easy management of child accounts.

Who Should Choose Dropbox Family?

If multiple members of your household need cloud storage, the Family plan offers excellent value. It simplifies account management while providing enough space for everyone's files.

Team and Business Plans

For businesses and teams, Dropbox offers robust plans that prioritize collaboration, security, and scalability.

1. Dropbox Standard

- **Storage:** 5 TB shared among team members.
- **Team Features:** Centralized admin controls, shared team folders, and activity monitoring.
- **Collaboration Tools:** Integration with Microsoft Office, Google Workspace, and other productivity tools.

2. Dropbox Advanced

- **Customizable Storage:** Scalable storage to meet your team's needs.
- **Enhanced Security:** Advanced encryption, single sign-on (SSO), and audit logs.
- **Collaboration Tools:** Team-based permissions and real-time file locking.

Who Should Choose Team and Business Plans?

These plans are ideal for startups, medium-sized businesses, and enterprise teams requiring a collaborative workspace with enhanced security and control. Dropbox Advanced, in particular, is well-suited for industries like finance, legal, and healthcare that deal with sensitive data.

Factors to Consider When Choosing a Plan

Choosing the right Dropbox plan requires understanding your storage, collaboration, and security needs. Here are some factors to guide your decision:

1. **Storage Requirements:**

   Evaluate the size and number of files you plan to store. If you frequently handle large media files, you'll need at least 2 TB of storage.

2. **Collaboration Needs:**

   Teams and businesses should prioritize plans with advanced collaboration tools like shared folders and file activity tracking.

3. **Budget:**
   Balance features with affordability. Individual plans like Dropbox Plus offer robust features at a reasonable cost, while business plans provide excellent value for organizations.

4. **Integration:**
   Check for compatibility with tools you already use, such as Google Workspace, Microsoft Office, or project management platforms like Trello.

5. **Security:**
   Users handling sensitive data should consider plans offering advanced security measures, such as Dropbox Advanced or higher-tier options.

Making the Most of Your Plan

Regardless of the plan you choose, here are some tips to maximize your Dropbox experience:

- **Use Smart Sync:** Keep your device storage optimized by syncing only the files you need.

- **Leverage Sharing Controls:** Protect your shared files with passwords and expiration dates.

- **Collaborate with Dropbox Paper:** Create and manage projects collaboratively in a single workspace.

By thoughtfully selecting a plan that aligns with your needs, you can unlock the full potential of Dropbox for both personal and professional use.

1.1.3 Understanding Storage Limits

Dropbox offers various plans to cater to the diverse needs of its users, ranging from personal to professional use. Each plan comes with specific storage limits and features. Understanding these limits is essential for efficient use of the platform, as it helps you choose the right plan, organize files effectively, and avoid unexpected restrictions.

Free Plan: Dropbox Basic

The **Dropbox Basic** plan is perfect for individuals new to cloud storage who need a simple way to manage personal files. It provides **2 GB of free storage**, which is sufficient for light use, such as storing text documents, PDFs, and a modest number of photos.

However, the 2 GB limit can be reached quickly if you store larger files like videos or high-resolution images. To monitor your usage:

- Navigate to the **Account Settings** page.
- Check the storage bar to see how much space you've used.
- Consider organizing files into folders and deleting unused files to free up space.

Tip: If you're running low on storage, Dropbox offers referral incentives. Inviting friends to join Dropbox can earn you up to **16 GB** of extra space.

Paid Plans: More Storage, More Features

Dropbox offers several paid plans tailored to individual and business needs. These plans come with enhanced storage and advanced features:

1. **Dropbox Plus**
    - **Storage:** 2 TB (2,000 GB)
    - **Ideal for:** Individuals with moderate to high storage needs, such as freelancers or photographers.
    - **Key Features:**
        - Offline access to files.
        - Smart Sync to save space on your device.
        - Rewind to undo changes to your account from the last 30 days.

2. **Dropbox Family**
    - **Storage:** 2 TB (shared among up to 6 users).
    - **Ideal for:** Families or groups needing shared storage.
    - **Key Features:**
        - Individual accounts for each user.
        - A Family Room folder for shared files.

3. **Dropbox Professional**
    - **Storage:** 3 TB (3,000 GB).
    - **Ideal for:** Professionals with advanced needs, like designers or video editors.
    - **Key Features:**
        - Advanced sharing controls.
        - Priority chat support.
        - Custom branding for shared files.

Business Plans: Tailored for Teams

For businesses and teams, Dropbox offers scalable storage options:

1. **Dropbox Standard**
    - **Storage:** 5 TB (shared among team members).
    - **Ideal for:** Small businesses with collaborative needs.
    - **Key Features:**
        - Team folders for centralized file management.
        - Admin tools for user activity monitoring.

2. **Dropbox Advanced**
    - **Storage:** As much as your team needs.
    - **Ideal for:** Growing businesses with high storage demands.
    - **Key Features:**
        - Advanced admin controls.
        - Data loss prevention (DLP) features.

3. **Dropbox Enterprise**
    - **Storage:** Customizable.
    - **Ideal for:** Large organizations with specialized requirements.

- **Key Features:**
    - Enterprise-grade security.
    - Dedicated customer support.

Storage Optimization Tips

Regardless of your plan, optimizing storage is key to maintaining an organized and efficient Dropbox account. Here are some practical strategies:

1. **Use Smart Sync**
    - Available for Plus, Professional, and Business users, **Smart Sync** allows you to access all your files without storing them locally on your device.
    - Mark files as "online-only" to save space.

2. **Compress Large Files**
    - Use tools like WinRAR or 7-Zip to compress files before uploading them.

3. **Delete Unnecessary Files Regularly**
    - Set a routine to review and delete files you no longer need.
    - Use the **Deleted Files** section to restore files within 30 days, or longer if you have a paid plan.

4. **Archive Old Projects**
    - Move completed projects to an external hard drive or another cloud service if they are no longer actively used.

5. **Monitor File Sizes**
    - Large files like videos can quickly consume your storage. Dropbox's **File Size Viewer** helps identify files that take up the most space.

Understanding Shared Space Usage

When you share files or folders, the space they occupy affects the storage of all users involved. For example:

- If a shared folder contains 1 GB of files, each participant sees a 1 GB reduction in their available storage.

- To avoid issues, consider sharing files via links instead of folders.

Upgrading When Needed

If you frequently encounter storage limitations, upgrading to a higher-tier plan ensures you can keep using Dropbox without disruptions. Dropbox makes it easy to upgrade directly from the app or website. Paid plans offer added value, such as priority support, advanced sharing options, and unlimited device linking.

By understanding Dropbox's storage limits and optimizing your usage, you can make the most of your plan while avoiding the frustration of running out of space. Whether you stick with the Basic plan or upgrade to a paid tier, having a clear strategy for managing your storage ensures a seamless Dropbox experience.

1.2 Installing Dropbox on Your Devices

1.2.1 Desktop Installation

Installing Dropbox on your desktop is the first step to seamlessly integrating cloud storage into your daily workflow. Whether you are a Windows or Mac user, Dropbox provides a streamlined installation process to ensure quick and efficient setup. This section will guide you through every step of the installation process, including downloading the software, installing it on your system, and customizing it to suit your preferences.

Step 1: Checking System Requirements

Before installing Dropbox, ensure your computer meets the minimum system requirements:

- **Operating System**: Windows 10 or later, macOS 10.14 (Mojave) or later.
- **Processor**: 1GHz or faster.
- **Memory**: At least 2GB of RAM.
- **Storage Space**: Minimum 500MB of available disk space for the application.

Having these requirements in place ensures smooth installation and optimal performance.

Step 2: Downloading the Dropbox Installer

To get started:

1. Open your web browser and navigate to the Dropbox download page.

2. Select the appropriate version for your operating system. Dropbox will automatically detect your OS, but you can manually select "Download for Windows" or "Download for macOS" if needed.

3. Save the installer file to a location where you can easily access it, such as the Desktop or Downloads folder.

Step 3: Running the Installer

Once the installer is downloaded:

1. **For Windows Users**: Double-click the .exe file to launch the installation wizard.

2. **For Mac Users**: Open the .dmg file, then drag and drop the Dropbox icon into the Applications folder.

Follow the on-screen instructions to proceed.

Step 4: Logging Into Your Account

After installation:

1. Open the Dropbox application.

2. Enter your login credentials (email and password). If you don't have an account yet, click "Sign Up" to create one.

3. Grant permissions for Dropbox to integrate with your system, such as allowing access to files and folders.

Step 5: Configuring Sync Settings

Dropbox syncs files between your computer and the cloud, but you can customize this process to optimize storage and bandwidth:

1. **Selective Sync**:
   - Go to the Preferences menu (accessible via the gear icon or the application's menu bar).
   - Select the "Sync" tab.
   - Choose "Selective Sync" to specify which folders to sync to your desktop. This is especially useful if you have limited hard drive space.

2. **Bandwidth Management**:
   - In the same Preferences menu, navigate to the "Network" tab.
   - Set upload and download rates to limit how much bandwidth Dropbox uses during syncing.

3. **Smart Sync (for Professional Plans)**:
   - Enable Smart Sync to keep files stored in the cloud and save local storage space. You can access these files on-demand.

Step 6: Exploring the Desktop Interface

Once Dropbox is installed and configured:

1. Locate the Dropbox folder on your computer.
   - For Windows: It's under the "This PC" or "Quick Access" section.
   - For Mac: You'll find it in the Finder's Favorites sidebar.
2. Files added to this folder automatically sync to the cloud and other connected devices.

3. Use the system tray (Windows) or menu bar (Mac) Dropbox icon to access shortcuts, such as viewing recent activity, pausing syncing, or opening preferences.

Step 7: Testing Your Installation

To confirm the setup is working correctly:

1. Drag and drop a test file into the Dropbox folder.

2. Check the status icons next to the file. A green checkmark indicates the file has synced successfully.

3. Log into your Dropbox account in a web browser and verify the file appears there.

Tips for Optimizing the Desktop Installation Experience

1. **Stay Updated**: Ensure the Dropbox app is always up to date by enabling automatic updates in the Preferences menu.

2. **Enable Notifications**: Configure desktop notifications to stay informed about file changes or sharing requests.

3. **Shortcuts for Efficiency**: Use keyboard shortcuts, such as Ctrl + Shift + D (Windows) or Command + Shift + D (Mac), to quickly open the Dropbox folder.

Troubleshooting Common Issues

- **Installation Fails**: Ensure no security software or firewalls are blocking the installer. Temporarily disable antivirus software if necessary.

- **App Doesn't Open**: Restart your computer and try again. If the problem persists, reinstall Dropbox.

- **Files Not Syncing**: Verify that your internet connection is stable and that there's sufficient storage space on your computer and Dropbox account.

By completing the desktop installation, you're equipped with a robust tool for managing files effortlessly across devices. The next section, **1.2.2 Mobile App Installation**, will guide you through bringing Dropbox's convenience to your smartphone or tablet.

1.2.2 Mobile App Installation

Dropbox's mobile app is a versatile tool that allows you to manage your files, collaborate with others, and stay organized on the go. Installing the app on your mobile device is straightforward, but there are essential steps to ensure proper setup and usage. This section provides a detailed guide to help you install the Dropbox app on both iOS and Android devices and customize it to fit your needs.

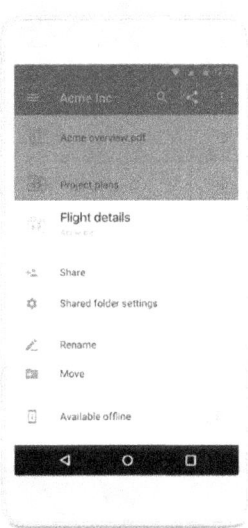
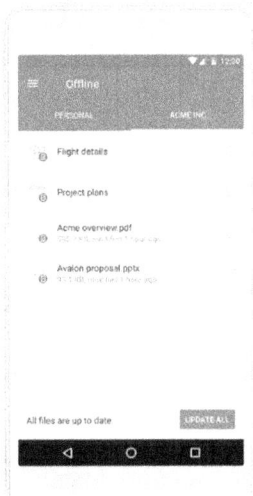

Step 1: Downloading the App

1. **Access Your App Store**

    o   For iOS users, open the **App Store** on your iPhone or iPad.

    o   For Android users, open the **Google Play Store** on your device.

2. **Search for Dropbox**

- Type "Dropbox" into the search bar. The app, identified by its blue box logo, should appear as one of the top results.

3. **Check the Developer**
    - Ensure the app is published by "Dropbox, Inc." to avoid downloading unofficial or unsafe versions.

4. **Initiate the Download**
    - Tap the "Get" button (iOS) or the "Install" button (Android).
    - Depending on your device settings, you may be asked to authenticate using Face ID, a fingerprint scan, or a password.

5. **Wait for Installation**
    - The app will download and install automatically. Once completed, its icon will appear on your home screen or in the app drawer.

Step 2: Logging into Dropbox

1. **Launch the App**
    - Open the Dropbox app by tapping its icon.

2. **Enter Your Credentials**
    - On the login screen, input your registered email address and password.
    - If you don't have an account yet, you can quickly sign up by selecting "Sign Up" and following the on-screen instructions.

3. **Enable Two-Factor Authentication (Optional)**
    - For enhanced security, activate two-factor authentication. This will require entering a code sent to your phone whenever you log in on a new device.

4. **Grant Permissions**
    - The app may request access to your camera, contacts, and files. Approve these permissions to use features like file uploads and sharing directly from your device.

Step 3: Configuring Basic Settings

1. **Choose Sync Preferences**
   - Decide if you want your photos, videos, or other files to automatically sync with Dropbox. You can adjust this later in the settings.

2. **Set Up Notifications**
   - Enable push notifications to stay updated on file activity, such as shared folder updates or edits made by collaborators.

3. **Select Offline Access Files**
   - Identify which files or folders you need offline. Dropbox will download them to your device so you can view them without internet access.

Step 4: Exploring the Mobile App Interface

1. **Home Tab**
   - This tab provides an overview of your most recent files, starred documents, and quick actions like creating new folders.

2. **Files Tab**
   - Access all your stored files and folders. You can sort, rename, or delete them directly within the app.

3. **Create Button**
   - Found at the bottom of the interface, this button lets you quickly upload files, scan documents, or create folders.

4. **Account Tab**
   - Manage your account settings, including subscription details, storage usage, and linked devices.

Troubleshooting Common Issues

1. **App Not Downloading**
   - Ensure your device has a stable internet connection. Check for available storage space and confirm your operating system is compatible with the Dropbox app.

2. **Login Problems**
   - Verify your email and password. If needed, use the "Forgot Password" feature to reset your credentials.

3. **Sync Delays**
   - Check your internet connection and ensure background app refresh is enabled for Dropbox.

4. **Permissions Denied**
   - Go to your device's settings and manually grant the app permissions for files, camera, or contacts.

Advanced Tips for Mobile Users

1. **Scanning Documents**
   - The Dropbox mobile app includes a document scanning feature. Open the app, tap the "Create" button, and select "Scan Document." This is useful for digitizing receipts, contracts, or notes.

2. **Sharing Files Directly from Mobile**
   - Long-press a file in the app to open sharing options. You can send a link via email, messaging apps, or social media.

3. **Customizing Notifications**
   - In the app's settings, choose which types of notifications you receive, such as comments on shared files or folder updates.

4. **Using Third-Party Integrations**
   - Link Dropbox with productivity apps like Slack or Zoom to streamline workflows directly from your mobile device.

Why Use the Mobile App?

The Dropbox mobile app isn't just a scaled-down version of its desktop counterpart; it's a robust tool designed to keep your files accessible wherever you are. Whether you're scanning documents on the fly, collaborating with a remote team, or reviewing presentations during your commute, the mobile app ensures that Dropbox is always at your fingertips.

With your app installed and set up, you're now ready to explore its powerful features and maximize your productivity. The next section will guide you through navigating Dropbox's interface to ensure you're making the most of its capabilities.

1.2.3 Configuring Sync Settings

Dropbox's ability to synchronize files across multiple devices is one of its most powerful features, enabling seamless access to your data wherever you are. Configuring sync settings properly is essential for optimizing your Dropbox experience, ensuring efficiency, and preventing unnecessary bandwidth or storage usage. In this section, we'll delve into the steps and best practices for configuring sync settings across desktop, mobile, and web platforms.

Understanding Dropbox Sync

The core of Dropbox sync lies in its ability to automatically update and store changes made to files or folders on one device and reflect those changes across all connected devices. This functionality is critical for collaborative workflows and personal organization. Before diving into specific settings, here's an overview of how Dropbox sync works:

1. **File Updates:** When a file is added, edited, or deleted in your Dropbox folder, the changes are immediately uploaded to Dropbox's servers and distributed to other connected devices.

2. **Selective Sync:** This feature allows users to choose specific folders to sync with their devices, conserving local storage.

3. **Smart Sync:** Available to paid plan users, Smart Sync extends Selective Sync by allowing files to appear on your device as placeholders without using local storage.

Configuring Sync Settings on Desktop

Step 1: Accessing Sync Preferences

To begin configuring your sync settings on a desktop:

1. Click on the Dropbox icon in your system tray (Windows) or menu bar (Mac).
2. Select the gear icon (⚙) to open the settings menu.
3. Navigate to the **Preferences** section, and then click on the **Sync** tab.

Step 2: Using Selective Sync

Selective Sync allows you to manage which folders are downloaded to your local device:

1. Within the **Sync** tab, locate the **Selective Sync** button.
2. A list of all folders in your Dropbox account will appear.
3. Uncheck the folders you don't want to sync to your device.
4. Click **Update** to apply the changes.

Tip: For large Dropbox accounts, unchecking infrequently used folders can free up significant local storage while retaining access to those files through the Dropbox web interface.

Step 3: Enabling Smart Sync (Paid Plans)

If you have a paid Dropbox plan, Smart Sync is a valuable tool for managing local storage:

1. Right-click on a file or folder in your Dropbox folder.
2. Hover over **Smart Sync**, and select one of the following:
    - **Online-Only:** Files are stored in the cloud but remain visible on your local drive.
    - **Local:** Files are fully downloaded to your device and available offline.

3. You can also configure default Smart Sync behavior from the **Preferences** menu.

Step 4: Managing Bandwidth

To optimize sync speed, you can adjust Dropbox's bandwidth usage:

1. In the Preferences menu, navigate to the **Bandwidth** section.

2. Set upload and download speed limits, or let Dropbox manage this automatically.

3. Limiting bandwidth may be helpful if you're working on a network with limited resources.

Configuring Sync Settings on Mobile Devices

Step 1: Accessing Sync Preferences

Sync settings on mobile devices are more streamlined but still offer powerful options:

1. Open the Dropbox mobile app.

2. Tap the menu icon (≡) and navigate to **Settings**.

Step 2: Enabling Offline Access

Offline access is crucial for users who work in environments with limited connectivity:

1. Navigate to the file or folder you want to access offline.

2. Tap the three dots (⋮) next to the item and select **Make Available Offline**.

3. These items will now be downloaded to your device.

Tip: Keep an eye on your device's storage, as offline files can quickly consume space.

Step 3: Configuring Camera Uploads

Dropbox's camera upload feature can automatically sync photos and videos:

1. In the **Settings** menu, toggle on **Camera Uploads**.

2. Choose whether to upload over Wi-Fi only or include mobile data.

3. Select if videos should be included or limited to photos only.

Configuring Sync Settings on the Web

While Dropbox's web platform doesn't involve local syncing, it offers critical tools for managing synced devices and controlling account-wide settings:

Step 1: Managing Linked Devices

1. Log in to Dropbox via the web.

2. Navigate to your **Account Settings** and select the **Security** tab.

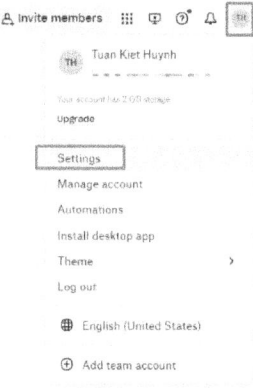

3. Under **Devices**, review and unlink any devices no longer in use to enhance security.

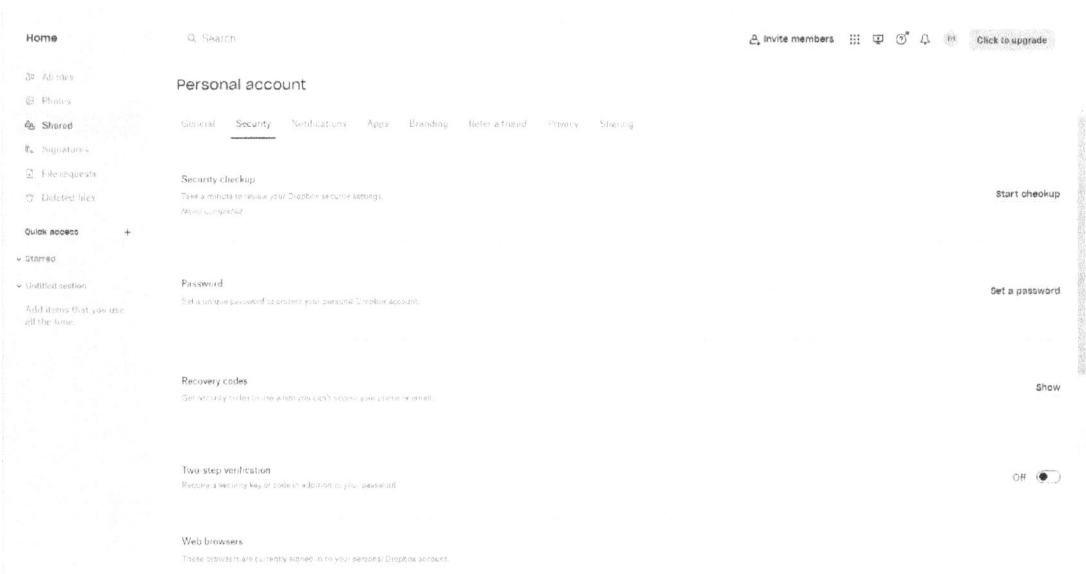

Devices
You haven't linked any devices to your personal Dropbox account. Install Dropbox to sync your devices.

Step 2: Clearing Space with Remote Delete

If a device is lost or stolen, Dropbox's **Remote Delete** feature allows you to protect your data:

1. From the web interface, go to **Account Settings** > **Security**.

2. Locate the device in question and choose **Delete Files** to remove synced files from the lost device.

Best Practices for Sync Optimization

1. **Regularly Audit Synced Folders:** Ensure that you're syncing only the folders you need on each device.

2. **Use Placeholder Files with Smart Sync:** Reduce local storage usage by utilizing online-only files.

3. **Monitor Bandwidth Usage:** Adjust bandwidth settings if you're experiencing slow network speeds.

4. **Stay Organized:** Create a folder structure that reflects your workflow for easier selective syncing.

Troubleshooting Common Sync Issues

Problem: Syncing is Slow

- Check your internet connection and bandwidth settings.
- Verify that no large files are clogging the upload queue.

Problem: Files Aren't Syncing

- Ensure the Dropbox app is running and signed in.
- Check that the folder isn't excluded via Selective Sync.

Problem: Device Storage is Full

- Use Smart Sync or adjust Selective Sync to limit local storage usage.

By following these steps and best practices, you can customize Dropbox's sync settings to suit your needs, maximize efficiency, and make the most of your cloud storage experience.

1.3 Navigating the Interface

1.3.1 Desktop Interface Overview

Dropbox's desktop interface is designed for simplicity and efficiency, allowing users to seamlessly manage their files and folders. Whether you're new to Dropbox or transitioning from another platform, understanding the layout and features of the desktop client is crucial to optimizing your experience. This section provides a detailed walkthrough of the key components and functionalities available in the Dropbox desktop interface.

1. Layout Overview

When you open the Dropbox application on your computer, the first thing you'll notice is its clean and minimalistic design. The interface consists of three main sections:

- **Navigation Sidebar**: Located on the left, this section provides quick access to key areas such as your files, shared folders, and recently accessed items.

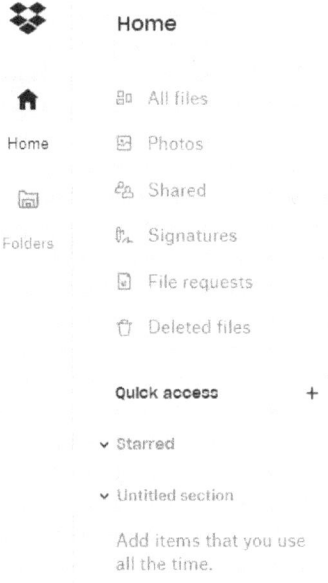

- **Main Workspace**: Occupying the center of the screen, this is where your files and folders are displayed.

- **Toolbar**: Positioned at the top or side (depending on the version), the toolbar offers shortcuts for common actions like uploading files, creating new folders, and adjusting settings.

2. Exploring the Navigation Sidebar

The navigation sidebar is your gateway to all the essential areas in Dropbox. Here's a breakdown of its components:

- **Home**:
  The "Home" tab gives you an overview of your recent activity. This includes recently added files, shared items, and suggestions based on your usage patterns. It's a great place to quickly resume work on something you've been editing.

  Home

- **Files**:
  This section displays all your files and folders stored in Dropbox. You can navigate through your folder structure here, open files directly, or right-click to perform actions like renaming, moving, or deleting.

  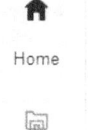
  Folders

- **Recents**:
  The "Recents" tab is a chronological list of files you've interacted with. It's perfect for quickly finding something you recently opened, uploaded, or edited.

- **Shared**:
  Under the "Shared" tab, you'll find all the files and folders that you've shared with others or that have been shared with you. This section provides tools for managing permissions and viewing shared activity.

- **Deleted Files**:

- This area lets you recover files that you've deleted within the last 30 days (or longer if you're on a premium plan). Simply select a file and click "Restore" to bring it back.

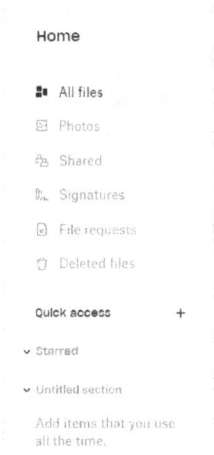

3. Navigating the Main Workspace

The main workspace is where your files and folders are displayed. Here are the key elements to understand:

- **File and Folder View**:

  Files and folders are displayed in either a list or grid view, depending on your preference. You can toggle between these views using the icon in the top-right corner of the workspace.

- **File Previews**:

  For many file types, Dropbox allows you to preview the content without opening it in another application. This is especially useful for images, PDFs, and Microsoft Office files.

- **Drag-and-Drop Functionality**:

  You can easily move files and folders by dragging them to a new location. This intuitive feature makes reorganizing your storage quick and easy.

4. Toolbar Features and Shortcuts

The toolbar at the top provides quick access to essential functions:

- **Upload Button**:

  Click this to upload files or folders directly from your computer to Dropbox.

- **New Folder**:

  Create a new folder to organize your files with a single click.

- **Search Bar**:

  The search functionality in Dropbox is powerful. You can search by file name, file type, or keywords within documents.

- **Settings and Preferences**:

  Access settings to adjust sync preferences, change your account details, or enable/disable desktop notifications.

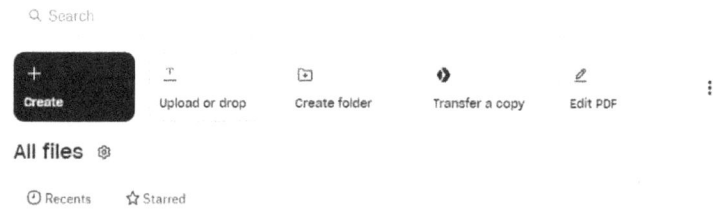

5. File Management Tools

Managing files is a breeze with the tools available in the desktop interface.

- **Right-Click Menu**:

Right-clicking on a file or folder opens a context menu with options such as "Share," "Download," "Rename," and "Move."

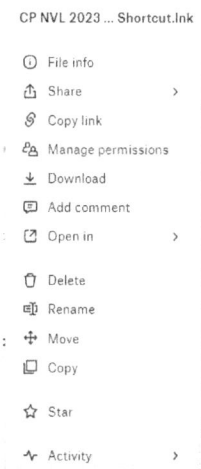

- **Starred Files**:

  Mark important files or folders as "starred" for quick access. Starred items are displayed prominently in a dedicated section in the sidebar.

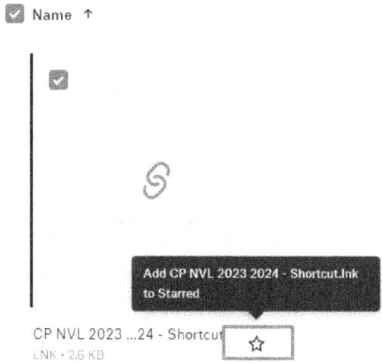

- **Batch Actions**:

  Select multiple files or folders to perform batch actions like deleting, moving, or sharing.

6. Integration with File Explorer/Finder

One of the standout features of the Dropbox desktop client is its integration with your computer's file management system (e.g., File Explorer on Windows or Finder on macOS).

- **Dropbox Folder**:

    Once installed, Dropbox creates a dedicated folder in your file manager. Any file or folder you place here is automatically synced with your cloud storage.

- **Status Indicators**:

    Each file and folder in your Dropbox folder has a status icon:

    - **Green Checkmark**: Fully synced.
    - **Blue Circle**: Sync in progress.
    - **Red X**: Sync error.

- **Right-Click Options**:

    From within File Explorer or Finder, you can right-click on a file to access Dropbox-specific actions like sharing or viewing version history.

7. Customizing Your Interface

Dropbox allows you to tailor the desktop interface to suit your workflow.

- **Changing View Settings**:

    Switch between list view and grid view, or adjust the size of thumbnails for better visibility.

- **Sorting Options**:

    Sort files by name, date modified, size, or type.

- **Dark Mode**:

    Enable dark mode to reduce eye strain, especially when working at night.

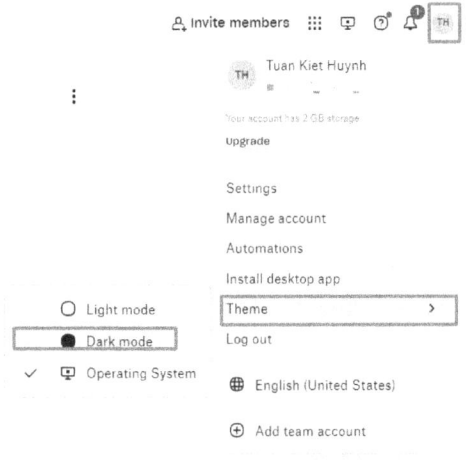

8. Tips for Efficient Navigation

- **Keyboard Shortcuts**:

    Familiarize yourself with Dropbox's keyboard shortcuts to speed up navigation. For example:

    - Press **Ctrl+F** (Windows) or **Command+F** (Mac) to open the search bar.
    - Use **Arrow Keys** to navigate between files and folders.

- **Pin Important Files**:

Use the "pin" feature to keep frequently used files at the top of your workspace.

- **Use Recent Files**:

    Leverage the "Recents" section to quickly access files you've worked on recently, saving time on navigation.

Conclusion

The Dropbox desktop interface is intuitive yet powerful, providing all the tools you need to manage your files effectively. By understanding its layout and features, you can streamline your workflow and make the most of what Dropbox offers. Up next, we'll dive into the mobile app interface to explore its unique features and capabilities.

1.3.2 Mobile App Navigation

Navigating Dropbox on your mobile device is a seamless experience, designed to provide quick access to your files anytime, anywhere. The mobile app offers a user-friendly interface that simplifies file management, collaboration, and sharing on the go. In this section, we'll walk you through the key features of the Dropbox mobile app and show you how to use them effectively.

Getting Familiar with the Mobile App Layout

When you open the Dropbox app, you'll be greeted with a clean, intuitive design. The main screen provides a high-level overview of your account and is divided into several key sections:

1. **Home Tab**:

    The Home tab serves as your dashboard, showcasing your most recently accessed files, starred items, and file activity. This makes it easy to pick up where you left off or quickly locate important files.

2. **Files Tab**:

    The Files tab is where all your folders and files are organized. You can view the folder structure exactly as it appears on your desktop or web app, making navigation consistent across devices.

3. **Search Bar**:

   Located at the top of the screen, the search bar is a powerful tool to find files and folders instantly. You can search by file name, file type, or even keywords within documents if you have an upgraded account with text recognition enabled.

4. **Create Button**:

   Positioned prominently, this button allows you to quickly create new files, upload photos, or scan documents.

5. **Account Settings**:

   Accessed from the profile icon, account settings let you manage preferences, such as notifications, offline files, and storage usage.

Exploring File and Folder Options

When you tap on a file or folder in the mobile app, a range of options is available:

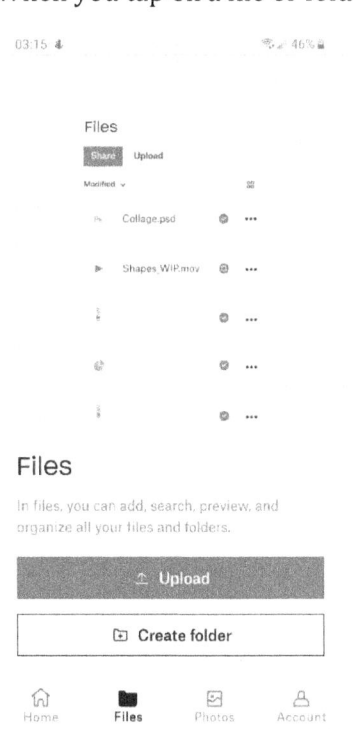

1. **Preview Files**:

   Tap a file to open and preview it within the app. Dropbox supports various file types, including PDFs, images, Word documents, and spreadsheets.

2. **File Actions**:

   Once you've opened or selected a file, you can perform actions like:

   - Renaming the file
   - Moving it to another folder
   - Marking it as a favorite for easy access
   - Sharing it with others

3. **Offline Access**:

   A standout feature of the mobile app is the ability to save files for offline use. This is particularly useful when you anticipate being without internet access. Simply toggle the "Available Offline" option, and the file will be downloaded to your device.

4. **Scanning Documents**:

    The mobile app includes a document scanning feature, allowing you to digitize paper documents using your phone's camera. The app can automatically crop and adjust the image for clarity.

Managing and Sharing Files on the Go

The Dropbox mobile app makes file management and sharing straightforward:

1. **Sharing Files and Folders**:

    Tap the "Share" button on any file or folder to generate a shareable link. You can customize permissions, allowing others to view, comment, or edit the file.

2. **Collaborative Features**:

    Use the "Add Comments" feature to collaborate with team members directly within the app. Comments are synced across all devices, ensuring everyone stays updated.

3. **Sorting and Filtering**:

    The app allows you to sort files by name, date modified, or size. You can also filter files to display only specific types, such as images, videos, or PDFs.

Customizing the Mobile App for Your Workflow

Dropbox's mobile app is highly customizable, enabling you to tailor it to your needs:

1. **Sync Settings**:

    Adjust sync settings to prioritize which files and folders are downloaded. This is useful if you have limited device storage.

2. **Notifications**:

    Enable or disable notifications for shared files, comments, and updates, ensuring you only receive alerts that are relevant to your workflow.

3. **Themes and Appearance**:

   Switch between light and dark mode for better visibility in different environments.

Troubleshooting Common Issues

Although the Dropbox mobile app is designed for reliability, occasional issues can arise. Here are some common problems and their solutions:

1. **Sync Delays**:
   - Ensure you have a stable internet connection.
   - Check that the app has permission to use mobile data in your device settings.

2. **Insufficient Storage**:
   - Delete unnecessary offline files to free up space.
   - Check your Dropbox storage quota to ensure you haven't exceeded your limit.

3. **App Crashes or Freezes**:
   - Update the app to the latest version.
   - Restart your device to clear temporary glitches.

Tips for Efficient Mobile Use

1. **Leverage Quick Actions**:

   Use long-press gestures to access quick actions like renaming or sharing files.

2. **Sync Frequently Used Files Offline**:

   Keep your most important files available offline for easy access without internet dependency.

3. **Integrate with Other Apps**:

Use Dropbox's integration with productivity apps like Microsoft Office and Adobe Acrobat to edit files directly from the mobile app.

By mastering Dropbox's mobile app, you'll unlock the full potential of cloud storage from your smartphone or tablet. Whether you're managing personal files, collaborating on team projects, or accessing documents on the move, the app is a vital tool for staying productive.

1.3.3 Key Features in the Web Version

Dropbox's web interface serves as the central hub for accessing your files, managing your account, and utilizing advanced features. While the desktop and mobile apps offer convenience and offline capabilities, the web version provides a streamlined experience that ensures your files are always accessible from any device with an internet connection. Let's explore the key features available in Dropbox's web interface, along with tips for maximizing their potential.

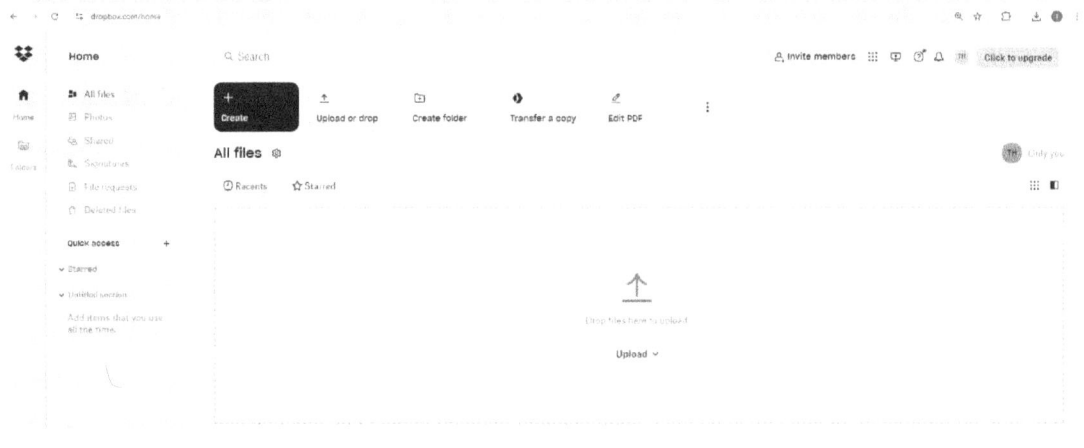

Accessing Your Files

The Dropbox web interface organizes your files in a way that's intuitive and user-friendly:
- **File Viewer:** The main dashboard displays your files and folders in a clear hierarchy. You can switch between list view and grid view, depending on your

preference. The search bar at the top allows for quick navigation to specific files or folders.

- **Recent Files:** The "Recent" tab highlights the files you've recently worked on, making it easy to pick up where you left off. This feature is especially useful for accessing files quickly without navigating through multiple folders.

- **Starred Items:** By starring files or folders, you can create a personalized list of favorites for fast access. Starred items are easily accessible from the left-hand menu.

File and Folder Management

The web interface is designed to simplify how you organize and manage your files:

- **Drag-and-Drop Functionality:** You can move files between folders directly from your browser. Dragging files from your computer into the web interface uploads them seamlessly.

- **Renaming and Deleting:** Right-clicking on a file or folder opens a context menu where you can rename, delete, or move items. Deleted files are sent to the "Deleted Files" section, where they can be restored within a specific time frame.

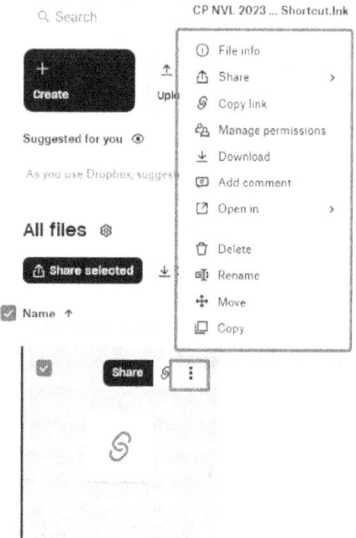

- **File Previews:** Dropbox supports previews for various file types, including PDFs, images, videos, and Microsoft Office documents. This eliminates the need to download files just to view their contents.

Sharing Files and Folders

One of Dropbox's standout features is its robust sharing capabilities:

- **Sharing Links:** You can create shareable links to files or folders directly from the web interface. These links can be sent to anyone, even if they don't have a Dropbox account.

- **Permission Settings:** The web version allows you to set permissions for shared files, such as view-only or edit access. Additionally, you can password-protect links or set expiration dates for added security.

- **Shared Folders:** Collaborating with others is made easy with shared folders. Invite team members or collaborators to a folder, granting them access to all contents within.

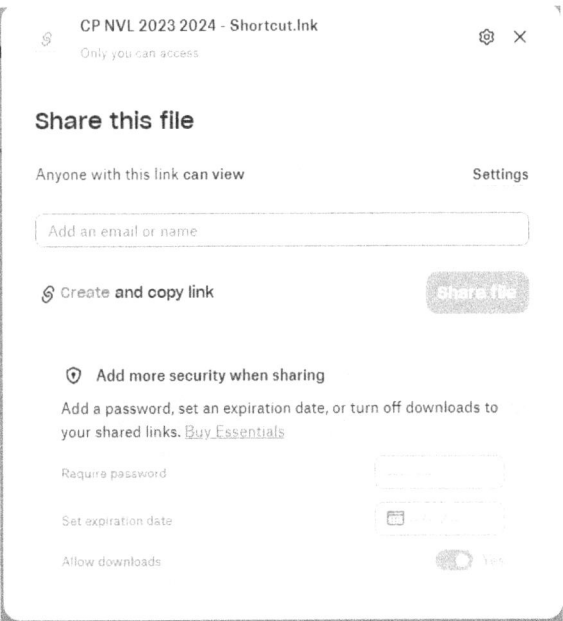

Collaboration Tools

The web version integrates several tools to facilitate collaboration and productivity:

- **Dropbox Paper:** Accessible from the left-hand menu, Dropbox Paper is a collaborative document-editing tool. It allows teams to co-edit documents in real time, add comments, and track changes.

- **Comments and Activity Feed:** You can comment directly on files to provide feedback or ask questions. The activity feed shows a history of changes made to files, helping teams stay aligned.

- **Requesting Files:** The "File Request" feature lets you collect files from others without giving them access to your Dropbox. This is particularly useful for projects requiring input from external contributors.

Version History and Recovery

Dropbox's version history feature ensures that accidental changes or deletions don't result in data loss:

- **Viewing Version History:** For any file, you can view previous versions by right-clicking and selecting "Version History." This feature is invaluable for recovering earlier drafts or undoing unwanted edits.

- **Restoring Deleted Files:** Deleted files are stored in the "Deleted Files" section, accessible from the left-hand menu. You can restore files within 30 days (or longer, depending on your plan).

Advanced Search and Filters

The search capabilities in the web version are designed to save you time:

- **Search Suggestions:** As you type into the search bar, Dropbox provides suggestions based on file names, extensions, and recent activity.

- **Filters:** You can narrow your search by file type (e.g., images, PDFs, videos), modification date, or who last edited the file.

- **Content Search (Pro and Business Plans):** Advanced search includes the ability to search within the content of documents, making it easier to locate specific information.

Account Settings and Preferences

The web interface also allows you to manage your account and preferences:

- **Account Overview:** The account settings page provides an overview of your storage usage, subscription plan, and connected devices.

- **Notification Preferences:** Customize your notifications to receive updates about shared files, collaboration activity, and more.

- **Linked Apps:** Manage third-party integrations, such as Google Workspace, Microsoft Office, or Trello, from the settings menu.

Integrations with Other Tools

Dropbox's web version supports seamless integrations with many popular tools:

- **Google Workspace and Microsoft Office:** Open and edit documents stored in Dropbox directly in Google Docs or Microsoft Office Online. Changes are saved automatically.

- **Slack Integration:** From the web interface, you can share files directly to Slack channels or messages.

- **Calendar Integration:** Link Dropbox to your calendar to attach files to meetings or events with ease.

Customizing the Web Interface

The web interface offers options for tailoring the layout and functionality to your needs:

- **Dark Mode:** Enable dark mode for a more comfortable viewing experience in low-light environments.

- **Keyboard Shortcuts:** Boost productivity by using keyboard shortcuts to navigate and perform actions quickly.

- **Pinned Folders:** Pin frequently used folders to the top of your dashboard for instant access.

Tips for Efficient Use

To make the most of Dropbox's web interface:

- **Bookmark Dropbox:** Bookmark the login page for quick access.

- **Offline Access:** For important files, enable offline access to ensure availability even without an internet connection.

- **Organizational Standards:** Set up consistent folder naming conventions and use tags for easy retrieval.

By understanding and utilizing the features of Dropbox's web interface, users can optimize their file management, collaboration, and productivity. Whether for personal use or professional projects, the web version serves as a reliable and powerful tool in the cloud storage ecosystem.

CHAPTER II
Uploading and Organizing Files

2.1 Uploading Files to Dropbox

2.1.1 Drag-and-Drop Uploads

Uploading files to Dropbox using the drag-and-drop feature is one of the simplest and most intuitive methods to move your files to the cloud. This section explores the step-by-step process, tips for optimizing your workflow, and troubleshooting common issues.

Overview of Drag-and-Drop Uploads

The drag-and-drop functionality allows users to upload files to Dropbox by simply selecting them from a location on their device and dragging them directly into the Dropbox interface. This feature is especially useful for individuals and teams handling multiple files daily, as it streamlines the upload process without requiring any complex technical steps.

CHAPTER II: UPLOADING AND ORGANIZING FILES

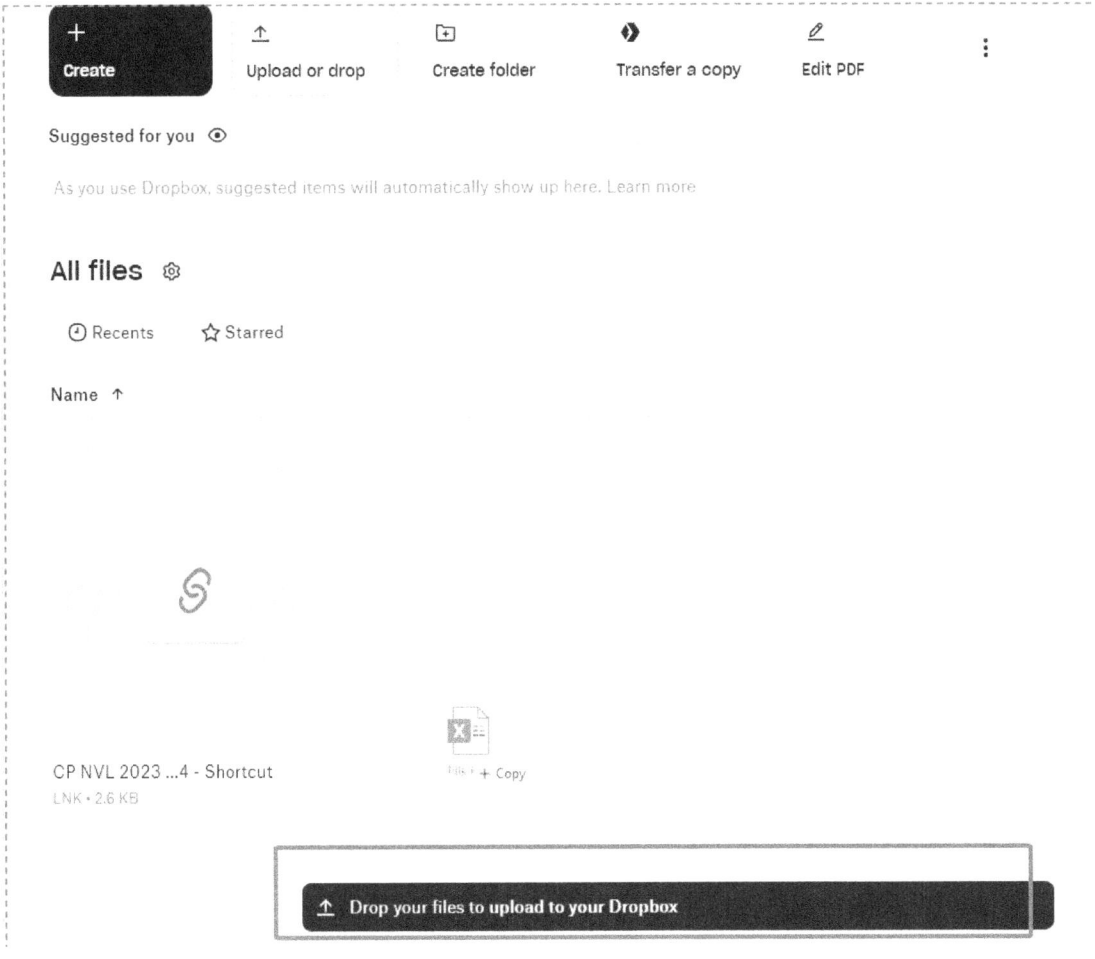

How to Use Drag-and-Drop on a Desktop Browser

1. **Log In to Dropbox:**

   Begin by logging into your Dropbox account on your preferred web browser. Ensure you are on the home screen or in the folder where you want to upload files.

2. **Locate Your Files:**

Open the file explorer (on Windows) or Finder (on macOS) and navigate to the files you wish to upload. Arrange your screen so both your file explorer and the Dropbox web page are visible.

3. **Drag and Drop:**

Click on the file(s) you want to upload and drag them over to the Dropbox folder in your web browser. As you hover, the interface will indicate where the files will be placed. Release the mouse button to start the upload.

4. **Monitor the Upload Progress:**

Dropbox will display an upload progress bar, showing the percentage of the transfer completed. Once the upload finishes, you'll see the files appear in the designated folder.

Using Drag-and-Drop with the Dropbox Desktop App

The Dropbox desktop app integrates with your computer's file system, making drag-and-drop even more seamless. Follow these steps to upload files:

1. **Open the Dropbox Folder:**

After installing the Dropbox desktop app, a dedicated Dropbox folder will appear on your computer. This folder syncs directly with your cloud storage.

2. **Select Files for Upload:**

Similar to the browser method, locate your files in your file explorer or Finder.

3. **Drag Files into the Dropbox Folder:**

Drag your selected files into the Dropbox folder. Once they are dropped in, the desktop app will automatically sync the files to the cloud.

4. **Check the Sync Status:**

The Dropbox desktop app uses status icons to show the progress of your upload. For example, a green checkmark indicates that a file has been successfully synced, while a blue circle means it's still in progress.

Tips for Efficient Drag-and-Drop Uploads

1. **Batch Upload Files:**

   Instead of uploading files individually, select multiple files at once to save time. Use the Ctrl (Windows) or Command (macOS) key to select multiple files.

2. **Organize Files Before Uploading:**

   Create folders on your device to group similar files. When you drag and drop, the entire folder structure will be replicated in Dropbox, ensuring better organization from the start.

3. **Use High-Speed Internet:**

   Large files or batches of files can take longer to upload, so ensure a stable and fast internet connection for smooth operation.

Troubleshooting Drag-and-Drop Issues

While drag-and-drop is designed to be user-friendly, occasional issues can arise. Here are some common problems and solutions:

1. **Files Not Uploading:**

   - **Cause:** This might occur due to a slow internet connection or a temporary glitch in the Dropbox web interface.
   - **Solution:** Check your internet connection and refresh the page. Alternatively, try the desktop app for a more reliable upload experience.

2. **Large Files Fail to Upload:**

   - **Cause:** Dropbox imposes file size limits based on your account type (e.g., Basic, Plus, or Professional).
   - **Solution:** Split the file into smaller parts using file compression tools or upgrade your Dropbox account for larger uploads.

3. **Drag-and-Drop Not Working in the Browser:**

   - **Cause:** Some older browsers may not fully support this functionality.

- **Solution:** Update your browser to the latest version or switch to a supported browser like Chrome, Firefox, or Edge.

4. **Sync Delays on the Desktop App:**

    - **Cause:** Syncing large files can take time, especially during peak usage hours.

    - **Solution:** Allow the app some time to complete the process. You can monitor sync progress using the app's status icon.

Use Cases for Drag-and-Drop Uploads

1. **Individual Users:**

   For personal use, drag-and-drop makes it easy to back up photos, videos, and documents from a computer to Dropbox in just seconds.

2. **Small Teams and Businesses:**

   Teams working on collaborative projects often need quick ways to share files. Drag-and-drop provides a simple solution for uploading drafts, presentations, and shared assets to team folders.

3. **Event Management:**

   Event planners can upload multiple photos or documents into shared Dropbox folders, ensuring all collaborators have immediate access.

Benefits of Drag-and-Drop Uploads

- **Speed and Convenience:** Drag-and-drop eliminates extra steps, allowing users to upload files in seconds.

- **Ease of Use:** Even individuals with minimal technical knowledge can master this feature effortlessly.

- **Compatibility:** Works seamlessly across operating systems and with most modern web browsers.

- **Real-Time Sync:** Files uploaded via drag-and-drop are immediately available across devices connected to your Dropbox account.

Conclusion

The drag-and-drop feature is a cornerstone of Dropbox's functionality, simplifying the file upload process for all users. Whether you're managing personal files or working on a team project, mastering this feature will save you time and effort. Next, we'll explore other methods of uploading files to Dropbox, ensuring you have a complete toolkit for managing your digital assets.

2.1.2 Uploading via Mobile App

Dropbox's mobile app is a powerful tool that allows you to access, upload, and manage your files on the go. Whether you're working from a smartphone or a tablet, this app ensures that you can seamlessly integrate your mobile workflow with your Dropbox account. In this section, we will explore the step-by-step process of uploading files using the mobile app, as well as tips to make the most out of this feature.

Getting Started with the Mobile App

Before uploading files via the mobile app, ensure you have the Dropbox app installed on your device. You can download it from the **Apple App Store** for iOS devices or **Google Play Store** for Android devices. Once installed, log in to your Dropbox account or create one if you're new to the platform.

Once logged in, you'll see the app's main interface, which typically includes tabs for Home, Files, Search, and Account. Familiarize yourself with these tabs, as they provide easy navigation through your account.

Steps to Upload Files Using the Mobile App

1. **Open the Dropbox App:**

CHAPTER II: UPLOADING AND ORGANIZING FILES

Launch the app on your mobile device. Navigate to the folder where you want to upload your files or create a new folder for better organization.

2. **Tap the '+' Button:**

   At the bottom of the screen, you'll find a circular **'+' button**. Tap this button to reveal a menu with several options, including **Upload files**, **Create or Upload folder**, **Take a photo**, and more.

   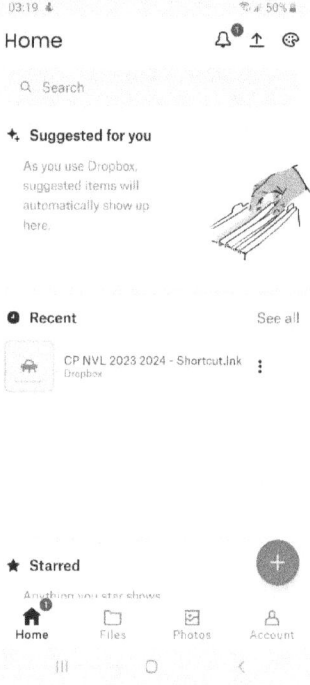

3. **Select 'Upload Files':**

   After tapping the **'+' button**, choose the **'Upload files'** option. This will open your device's file manager or gallery.

4. **Choose Your Files:**

   Browse through your device's storage to select the files you want to upload. You can select multiple files by long-pressing on one and then tapping on additional files.

5. **Confirm Upload Location:**

Once you've selected the files, confirm the folder in your Dropbox account where the files will be uploaded. If you're not in the desired folder, you can change the upload destination at this stage.

6. **Tap 'Upload':**

   After confirming the folder, tap the **'Upload'** button. The app will begin uploading your files to Dropbox. You'll see a progress bar or indicator to track the upload status.

Tips for Efficient Uploading

1. **Use Wi-Fi for Large Files:**

   Uploading large files can consume significant mobile data. Connect to a stable Wi-Fi network to avoid exceeding your data limits.

2. **Organize Before Uploading:**

   To save time later, organize your files into folders before uploading them to Dropbox. This makes it easier to locate and manage them in the future.

3. **Monitor Battery Usage:**

   Uploading large files can drain your device's battery. Ensure your phone or tablet is sufficiently charged or connected to a power source during uploads.

Uploading Photos and Videos

The Dropbox mobile app includes features tailored for photos and videos, making it a convenient option for backing up media files.

1. **Automatic Camera Uploads:**

   Enable the **Camera Uploads** feature to automatically back up photos and videos from your device to Dropbox. This setting can be turned on by navigating to the **Account Settings** in the app and selecting **Camera Uploads**.

2. **Manual Media Uploads:**

For selective uploads, open the app, tap the **'+' button**, and choose **'Upload photos'**. You can then pick specific images or videos from your gallery to upload.

3. **High-Quality Uploads:**

   Dropbox allows you to upload photos and videos in their original quality. To adjust this setting, go to **Account Settings** and ensure **High-Resolution Uploads** is enabled.

Using the 'Take a Photo' Feature

If you want to capture and upload a photo directly, the **'Take a Photo'** option in the **'+' menu** is your go-to tool. This feature is ideal for scanning documents, capturing receipts, or sharing real-time images with colleagues.

1. **Tap 'Take a Photo':**

   Choose the **'Take a Photo'** option from the **'+' menu**. This will activate your device's camera.

2. **Capture the Image:**

   Take a photo as you would normally. After capturing, you'll have the option to crop or adjust the image before uploading.

3. **Select Upload Destination:**

   Once satisfied with the image, confirm the upload folder and tap **'Upload.'**

Troubleshooting Upload Issues

1. **Insufficient Storage:**

   If you encounter an error stating **"Not enough storage space,"** check your Dropbox account's available storage. Consider upgrading to a larger plan or deleting unnecessary files.

2. **Network Errors:**

   Upload failures can occur due to poor internet connectivity. Ensure you're connected to a stable Wi-Fi network or have a strong mobile data signal.

3. **App Crashes or Freezes:**

   If the app crashes during an upload, restart it and try again. Updating the app to the latest version can also resolve performance issues.

Benefits of Uploading via Mobile App

1. **Convenience:**

   Uploading files via the mobile app eliminates the need for a computer, allowing you to manage your Dropbox account anytime, anywhere.

2. **Real-Time Collaboration:**

   Instantly share uploaded files with others, making it easier to collaborate on the go.

3. **Enhanced Accessibility:**

   Uploaded files are synced across all your devices, ensuring you can access them wherever you are.

By following these steps and tips, you can efficiently use the Dropbox mobile app to upload files, photos, and videos. This feature not only enhances productivity but also ensures your important files are securely stored and easily accessible.

2.1.3 Using the File Request Feature

Dropbox's **File Request** feature is a powerful tool designed to streamline the process of collecting files from multiple people, even those without a Dropbox account. This functionality is especially useful for businesses, educators, project managers, or anyone who needs to gather documents, images, or other files from various contributors without sending out multiple emails or links.

What is the File Request Feature?

The **File Request** feature allows you to create a secure and organized way for others to send you files directly into a specified Dropbox folder. Instead of users navigating complicated processes, they simply click a link you provide, upload their files, and the files appear neatly in your folder.

Key benefits of the File Request feature include:

- **Simplicity:** No Dropbox account is required for file senders.
- **Control:** You choose the destination folder in Dropbox where the uploaded files will go.
- **File Size:** Contributors can upload files as large as your storage limits allow.
- **Security:** Files are uploaded privately and securely.

How to Set Up a File Request

Step 1: Access the File Request Tool

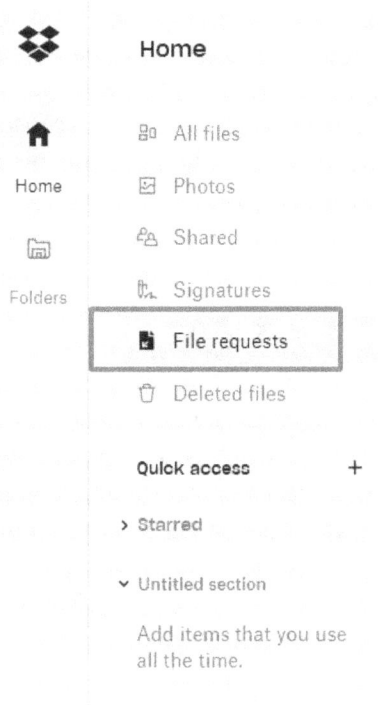

1. Open your Dropbox account and navigate to the **Home** or **Files** page.

2. On the left-hand menu, locate and click **File Requests**.

3. If you've never used the feature before, Dropbox will guide you through an introductory setup.

Step 2: Create a New File Request

1. Click the **Create File Request** button.

2. Fill out the request form:

    o **Title Your Request:** Provide a clear title, such as *"Submit Quarterly Reports"* or *"Upload Presentation Slides"*.

    o **Add a Description (Optional):** Include instructions or details about the type of files needed.

CHAPTER II: UPLOADING AND ORGANIZING FILES

3. Choose a destination folder in your Dropbox where the files will be stored. If a folder doesn't exist yet, you can create one directly from this step.

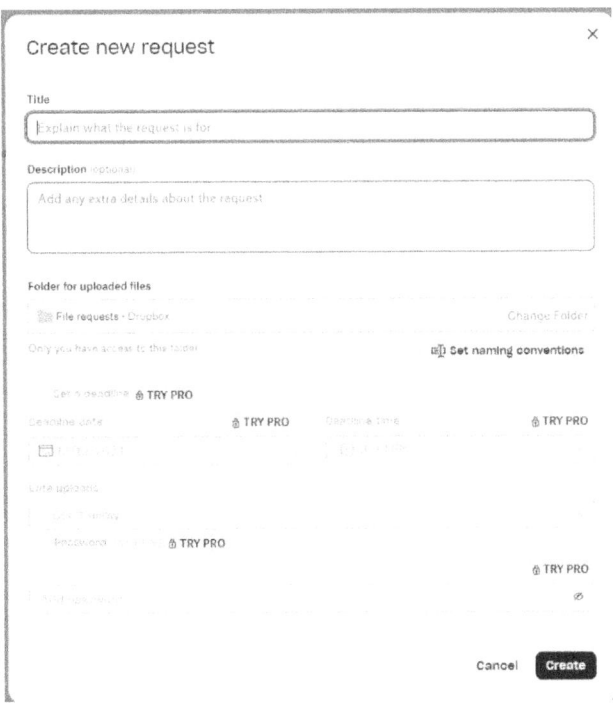

Step 3: Share the Request Link

1. Dropbox will generate a unique link for your file request.

2. Share this link via email, messaging apps, or embed it in a webpage.

3. Optionally, set a deadline for submissions, ensuring contributors submit files by a specific date.

Using the File Request Feature Effectively

To make the most of the File Request feature, follow these best practices:

1. Be Specific in Your Instructions

When creating a file request, clarity is crucial. Include detailed instructions about:

- The file format (e.g., PDF, Word document, JPEG).

- File naming conventions (e.g., *"LastName_ProjectName.pdf"*).
- Submission deadlines.

2. Organize by Folder

Assign a unique folder for each request to keep files separated and organized. For instance, if you're collecting event photos from multiple contributors, create a folder titled *"Event 2024 Photos"* rather than mixing these files with unrelated uploads.

3. Set Deadlines and Reminders

Deadlines ensure contributors submit files on time. Dropbox allows you to automate reminders, gently prompting users to upload files before the deadline.

4. Protect Your Storage Space

If you expect to receive a large volume of files, ensure you have sufficient storage available. Consider upgrading to a plan that accommodates the expected upload size if necessary.

How File Request Works for Contributors

Contributors will experience a straightforward process when responding to a File Request. Here's what they see:

1. They click the shared link, leading them to a web page with your instructions.
2. They upload their files by dragging and dropping them or selecting files from their device.
3. Once uploaded, they'll receive a confirmation that their files were successfully sent.

Use Cases for File Requests

1. Business Applications

- **Recruitment:** HR teams can gather resumes, cover letters, or certifications during hiring.

- **Client Documentation:** Businesses can collect contracts, invoices, or reports securely from clients.
- **Event Planning:** Collect photos, RSVPs, or other materials from event attendees.

2. Educational Purposes

- **Homework Submissions:** Teachers can request assignments from students.
- **Research Projects:** Researchers can collect data or contributions from collaborators.

3. Personal Use

- **Event Organization:** Gather photos, videos, or files after a family reunion or wedding.
- **Collaborative Projects:** Share a request link with friends for a group project or creative collaboration.

Managing File Requests

Viewing and Organizing Files

Once files are uploaded, you can view them directly in the designated Dropbox folder. Use file naming conventions or subfolders to keep everything tidy.

Editing or Closing a File Request

If you need to make changes to a file request:

1. Go to the **File Requests** section in Dropbox.
2. Locate the active request, and click **Edit**.
3. Adjust the title, description, or deadline as needed.
4. If the file collection is complete, close the request to prevent further uploads.

Troubleshooting File Request Issues

1. Contributors Unable to Upload Files

- Ensure the shared link is correct and active.
- Verify that your Dropbox account has enough storage space for uploads.

2. Files Not Appearing in the Designated Folder

- Check if the correct folder was selected during setup.
- Review the File Request settings to ensure no changes were made inadvertently.

3. Security Concerns

- If you suspect unauthorized access to your file request link, close it immediately and create a new one.

Conclusion

The **File Request** feature in Dropbox is an indispensable tool for collecting files from a diverse group of contributors, all while maintaining simplicity and security. Whether you're a professional managing client documents or an educator gathering assignments, this feature ensures a seamless and efficient file submission process. By following best practices, setting clear expectations, and staying organized, you'll unlock the full potential of Dropbox's File Request capabilities.

2.2 Creating and Managing Folders

2.2.1 Best Practices for Folder Organization

Organizing your files effectively within Dropbox is essential for maintaining productivity and ensuring that your data is easily accessible. With proper folder organization, you can avoid wasting time searching for files and reduce the risk of losing important documents. In this section, we will explore best practices for structuring your Dropbox folders, naming conventions, categorizing content, and maintaining a system that grows with your needs.

Start with a Logical Folder Structure

The foundation of good folder organization is creating a structure that makes sense to you and others who may access your Dropbox. Here are some tips to get started:

1. **Think Hierarchically**

   Design your folder structure to reflect a hierarchy, starting from broad categories and working down to more specific subcategories. For example:

   - Main Folder: *Work Projects*
     - Subfolder: *2024 Reports*
       - Subfolder: *Q1 Financials*

2. **Match the Nature of Your Files**

   Organize folders based on how you use your files. Common methods include organizing by:

   - **Date** (e.g., years, quarters, months)
   - **Project** (e.g., client names, task types)
   - **Purpose** (e.g., personal, work, hobbies)

3. **Limit Depth**

Avoid creating folders that are too deeply nested. While it might seem organized, it can become cumbersome to navigate. Instead, aim for a balance between structure and accessibility.

Use Descriptive Folder Names

Folder names are the key to quick identification of their contents. Here's how to make them more effective:

1. **Be Clear and Specific**

   Ambiguous folder names like "Miscellaneous" or "Stuff" should be avoided. Instead, use descriptive names like "Client Invoices 2024" or "Vacation Photos - Italy."

2. **Adopt Naming Conventions**
   Consistent naming conventions make it easier to locate and share files. Some popular systems include:

   - **Date-based Naming**: Use YYYY-MM-DD format for chronological order (e.g., *2024-01 Marketing Plan*).

   - **Category Prefixes**: Start with a general category, followed by specifics (e.g., *HR_Resumes_Jan2024*).

   - **Avoid Special Characters**: Special characters like "/" or "*" can cause compatibility issues. Stick to alphanumeric characters and underscores.

3. **Leverage Sorting Features**

   Alphabetize your folders by prefixing with numbers (e.g., "1_Work," "2_Personal"). This method ensures that frequently used folders appear at the top of your list.

Declutter and Consolidate Regularly

Over time, your Dropbox can become cluttered with outdated or redundant files. Make it a habit to:

1. **Review and Archive**

   Periodically review your folders to identify old files that can be archived. Dropbox's Archive feature allows you to store older files separately without deleting them.

2. **Merge Redundant Folders**

   If you find multiple folders with overlapping content, consolidate them into one. For example, if you have "Invoices_2023" and "Invoices_2024," consider merging them into a single folder named "Invoices."

3. **Delete Irrelevant Files**

   Unused or outdated files take up space and add unnecessary complexity. Regularly clean up folders by deleting these files.

Tagging and Folder Notes

While Dropbox itself doesn't support traditional "tags," you can still implement your own system:

1. **Use File Names as Tags**

   Add relevant keywords directly to file or folder names for easy searching. For example, instead of naming a file "Report.pdf," use "Sales_Report_2024_Q1.pdf."

2. **Add Descriptive Notes**

   Use file descriptions or README.txt files within folders to explain their purpose. This is particularly useful for shared folders where collaborators might need context.

Adopt Folder Templates for Recurring Projects

For recurring tasks or projects, create a folder template with pre-named subfolders to ensure consistency. For instance, a "Project Template" folder could include:

- "01_Research"
- "02_Design"

- "03_Execution"
- "04_Deliverables"

When starting a new project, simply duplicate the template and rename it accordingly.

Collaborate on Folder Organization

If you are sharing Dropbox with a team, ensure everyone is aligned on folder organization.

1. **Create a Team Policy**

    Draft guidelines on folder naming, hierarchy, and maintenance. For example, specify whether files should be categorized by department or client.

2. **Assign Folder Owners**

    For team folders, designate someone to oversee updates and ensure files are kept up-to-date.

3. **Use Shared Folders Wisely**

    Avoid overloading shared folders with irrelevant files. Encourage collaborators to only upload files that are necessary for the team.

Avoid Common Mistakes in Folder Organization

To maximize efficiency, steer clear of these pitfalls:

1. **Over-Categorization**

    Creating too many folders can lead to confusion. Keep your structure simple and intuitive.

2. **Duplicate Files**

    Storing the same file in multiple locations wastes space and creates confusion. Use links or shortcuts instead.

3. **Neglecting Updates**

An outdated system is almost as bad as no system at all. Commit to regular reviews and updates.

Utilize Dropbox Features for Organization

Dropbox offers built-in features that can enhance folder management:

1. **Starred Folders**

    Mark frequently accessed folders as "Starred" for quick access.

2. **Dropbox Smart Sync**

    Save local storage by setting rarely used folders to "Online-Only."

3. **Shared Folder Activity**

    Track changes to shared folders to ensure everyone stays informed.

By implementing these best practices, you can create a well-organized folder system in Dropbox that is both efficient and scalable. Whether you are managing personal files or collaborating with a team, a structured approach will save time and reduce stress. Stay consistent and regularly evaluate your setup to adapt to your evolving needs.

2.2.2 Renaming and Moving Files

Efficient file management is a cornerstone of using Dropbox effectively, and knowing how to rename and move files within your account can significantly improve your organization. This section delves into the processes, best practices, and common scenarios for renaming and relocating files in Dropbox.

Renaming Files in Dropbox

Renaming files in Dropbox is a straightforward process that allows you to clarify file names, correct errors, or adopt a naming convention for better organization.

How to Rename Files on the Dropbox Web Interface:

1. **Log in to Your Account:** Open your browser and go to Dropbox.com. Log in to your account if you aren't already.

2. **Locate the File:** Navigate to the folder where the file you want to rename is stored.

3. **Open the File Options:** Hover over the file and click on the three dots (ellipsis) to open the context menu.

4. **Select "Rename":** Choose the "Rename" option from the dropdown menu.

5. **Enter the New Name:** Type the desired name for your file and press Enter. The file name will update immediately.

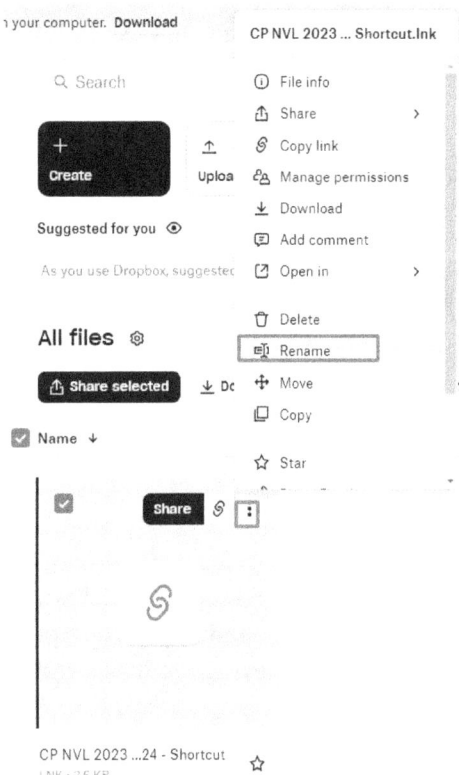

Renaming Files on the Dropbox Mobile App:

1. **Open the App:** Launch the Dropbox app on your smartphone or tablet.

2. **Find the File:** Navigate to the specific file you want to rename.

3. **Access File Options:** Tap on the three dots next to the file name to open the menu.

4. **Tap "Rename":** Select the "Rename" option.

5. **Input the New Name:** Enter the new file name in the dialog box and confirm.

Renaming Files on Desktop (via File Explorer or Finder): When you use the Dropbox desktop app, renaming files is no different from renaming files on your computer:

1. Open your Dropbox folder through File Explorer (Windows) or Finder (Mac).

2. Locate the file, right-click on it, and select "Rename."

3. Enter the new name and press Enter.

Best Practices for Renaming Files

Renaming files might seem trivial, but following a few best practices can make your workflow more efficient:

- **Use Descriptive Names:** Instead of "IMG1234.jpg," rename files to something more informative like "Vacation_Paris_2024.jpg."

- **Adopt a Naming Convention:** Consistency is key. Use formats like "YYYY-MM-DD_ProjectName_VersionNumber" for professional documents.

- **Avoid Special Characters:** Many systems struggle with special characters in file names. Stick to letters, numbers, underscores, and hyphens.

- **Use Search-Friendly Terms:** Consider what terms you might use later to search for the file, and incorporate those into the name.

Moving Files in Dropbox

Moving files is equally essential for maintaining an organized structure, enabling you to group related files or transfer them to shared folders for collaboration.

Moving Files on the Dropbox Web Interface:

1. **Locate the File:** Log in to your Dropbox account and navigate to the file you want to move.

2. **Open the File Options:** Click on the three dots next to the file name to access the menu.

3. **Select "Move":** Choose the "Move" option.

4. **Choose the Destination Folder:** Browse or search for the folder where you want to move the file.

5. **Confirm the Move:** Click "Move" to finalize the process.

Moving Files on the Dropbox Mobile App:

1. Open the app and locate the file.

2. Tap on the three dots next to the file name.

3. Select "Move to" from the menu.

4. Browse or search for the destination folder.

5. Tap "Move" to complete the action.

Moving Files on Desktop (via File Explorer or Finder):

1. Open the Dropbox folder on your computer.

2. Drag the file to the desired folder, or cut and paste it using keyboard shortcuts (Ctrl+X and Ctrl+V on Windows, Command+X and Command+V on Mac).

Common Scenarios for Moving Files

Understanding when and why you might move files can help you make better use of Dropbox's capabilities:

1. **Organizing Projects:** Keep all files for a specific project in one folder for easy access.

2. **Archiving Old Files:** Move older files to an "Archive" folder to declutter your workspace.

3. **Sharing Files:** Move files into shared folders to grant collaborators access.

4. **Merging Content:** Consolidate files from multiple folders into a single location for better organization.

Troubleshooting Renaming and Moving Files

While Dropbox is intuitive, you might occasionally encounter issues when renaming or moving files. Here are some common problems and solutions:

1. File is in Use:

If a file is open in another application, Dropbox may not allow renaming or moving until it's closed. Ensure all related applications are closed before trying again.

2. Permission Denied:

For shared files, ensure you have the correct permissions. Only owners or editors can rename or move shared files.

3. Syncing Issues:

If changes aren't reflected across devices, it could be a syncing issue. Check your internet connection and ensure the Dropbox app is running.

Conclusion

Mastering the art of renaming and moving files in Dropbox is a fundamental skill for effective cloud storage management. By adopting consistent naming conventions and keeping your folders organized, you'll not only streamline your workflow but also make your Dropbox account easier to navigate. Whether you're a casual user or managing files for a team, these techniques lay the groundwork for a productive and organized digital environment.

2.2.3 Deleting and Recovering Files

Efficiently managing your files in Dropbox includes knowing how to delete unneeded files and recover them if necessary. This section explores the processes for deleting files, understanding how deleted files are managed, and recovering them when required. Let's break it down step by step to ensure you can confidently manage these tasks.

Deleting Files in Dropbox

Deleting files in Dropbox is a straightforward process, whether you are using the desktop app, the mobile app, or the web interface. Here's how you can do it:

1. **Deleting Files via the Web Interface**

    o **Navigate to Your File**: Log into your Dropbox account on your web browser. Locate the file or folder you wish to delete.

    o **Right-Click or Use Options Menu**: Right-click on the file or folder and select "Delete" from the dropdown menu. Alternatively, use the three-dot menu on the right side of the file.

    o **Confirm Deletion**: A prompt will appear asking for confirmation. Click "Delete" to move the file to the Deleted Files folder.

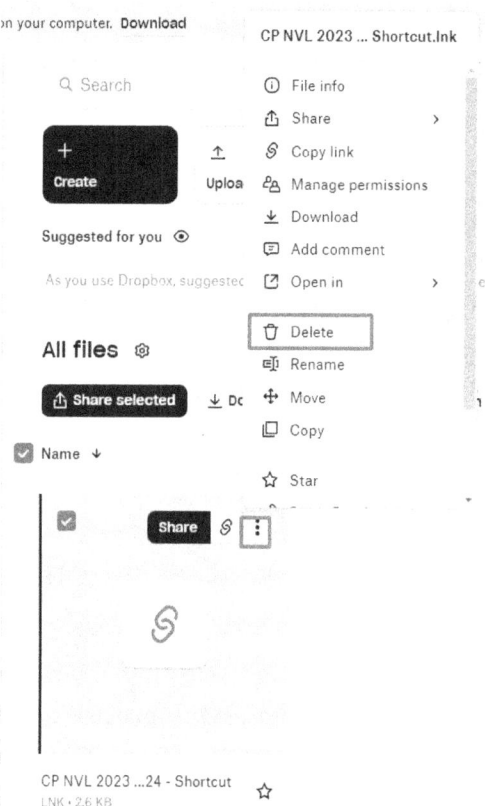

2. **Deleting Files via the Desktop App**

- **Find the File in Your Dropbox Folder**: Open your local Dropbox folder.
- **Drag to Recycle Bin or Trash**: Simply drag the file or folder to your computer's Recycle Bin (Windows) or Trash (Mac).
- **Sync Changes**: Dropbox automatically syncs the deletion, moving the file to the Deleted Files folder in the cloud.

3. **Deleting Files on Mobile**
   - **Open the App**: Launch the Dropbox mobile app and navigate to the file or folder.
   - **Select and Delete**: Tap the three-dot menu next to the file or folder and select "Delete." Confirm the deletion when prompted.

What Happens to Deleted Files?

When you delete a file in Dropbox, it doesn't vanish permanently. Instead, it is moved to the **Deleted Files** folder, where it is stored temporarily. This feature ensures that accidental deletions can be easily reversed.

- **Deleted Files Retention Period**:
  - For free (Basic) accounts, deleted files are stored for up to **30 days**.
  - For Professional and Business plans, files may be recoverable for up to **180 days**, depending on the account's settings.

- **Impact on Storage Space**:
  - Deleted files do not count toward your storage quota.
  - However, they are not permanently removed until the retention period ends or you manually empty the Deleted Files folder.

Recovering Deleted Files

Dropbox makes it simple to recover deleted files if you need them back. Here's how to do it on different platforms:

1. **Recovering via the Web Interface**

CHAPTER II: UPLOADING AND ORGANIZING FILES

- o **Access Deleted Files**: On the Dropbox homepage, click the "Deleted files" option on the left sidebar.

- o **Locate Your File**: Browse or use the search bar to find the file you want to restore.

- o **Restore the File**: Select the file and click "Restore." The file will be returned to its original location in your Dropbox.

2. **Recovering via Version History**

    - o **Right-Click on File**: If a file was modified before deletion, you can use the Version History feature to restore an earlier version. Right-click on the file and select "Version history."

    - o **Select a Version**: Choose the version you want and click "Restore."

3. **Recovering via the Desktop App**

    - o Unfortunately, the desktop app doesn't have a dedicated interface for deleted files. Use the web interface for recovery.

CHAPTER II: UPLOADING AND ORGANIZING FILES

4. **Recovering on Mobile**
    - **Navigate to Deleted Files**: Tap on the menu icon, then select "Deleted files."
    - **Select and Restore**: Locate the file, tap it, and select "Restore" to recover the file to its original location.

Permanently Deleting Files

If you need to remove files permanently from Dropbox (for privacy or space-saving reasons), follow these steps:

1. **Go to Deleted Files**: Navigate to the Deleted Files section via the web interface.
2. **Select Files for Permanent Deletion**: Highlight the files or folders you want to delete permanently.
3. **Click "Permanently Delete"**: Confirm the action to remove the files from Dropbox's servers.

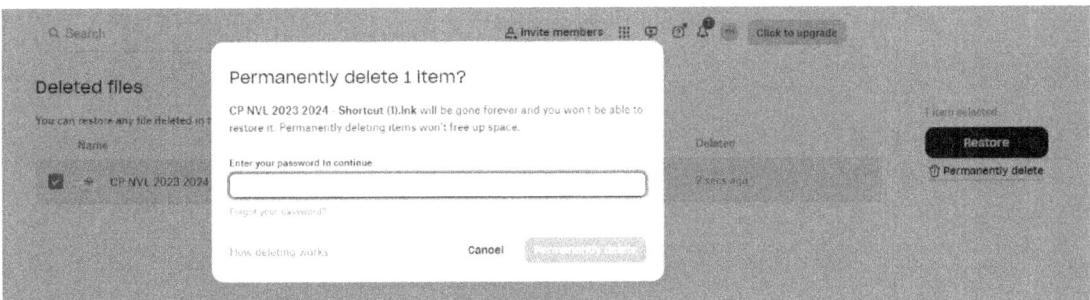

Note: Once a file is permanently deleted, it cannot be recovered. Use this option cautiously.

Best Practices for Managing Deleted Files

1. **Regular Cleanup**: Periodically review the Deleted Files folder to clear out unnecessary files, freeing up mental and digital space.
2. **Understand Retention Policies**: Familiarize yourself with Dropbox's retention limits based on your plan. Upgrade if you need extended recovery periods.

3. **Use Shared Folder Caution**: If you delete files from shared folders, they may affect collaborators. Communicate with your team before removing shared content.

4. **Enable Extended Version History**: For critical projects, consider enabling Dropbox's extended version history (if available) to ensure you have more time to recover files.

Troubleshooting File Deletion and Recovery Issues

If you encounter problems when trying to delete or recover files, here are some tips to resolve them:

- **Missing Files After Deletion**: Double-check the Deleted Files folder and any shared folder where the file might have been moved.

- **Unable to Restore**: Ensure your account is active and that the file is still within the retention period.

- **Contact Support**: If all else fails, Dropbox's support team can help locate and recover files under certain conditions.

By mastering the art of deleting and recovering files in Dropbox, you'll maintain an organized, clutter-free workspace while ensuring no critical files are lost permanently.

2.3 Searching for Files

2.3.1 Using the Search Bar

Searching for files efficiently is one of the key skills for maximizing productivity with Dropbox. Whether you're looking for a document you edited yesterday, an image you uploaded months ago, or a shared folder with collaborators, Dropbox's search bar is your gateway to quick and seamless file retrieval. In this section, we'll explore the ins and outs of using the search bar, tips for refining your queries, and ways to make the most of Dropbox's search features.

Understanding the Search Bar

The search bar in Dropbox is prominently located at the top of the interface in both the desktop application and the web version. It provides a unified way to search across all your files and folders, regardless of their location or type. By simply typing in a keyword, you can find files, folders, shared items, and even specific text within certain file types like PDFs and Word documents (if you have a Dropbox Pro or Business account).

Here's how the search bar works:

1. **Basic Keyword Search**: Enter a word or phrase related to the file or folder name. Dropbox will display results based on matches found in file names, folder titles, and metadata.

2. **Auto-Suggestions**: As you type, Dropbox provides real-time suggestions, showing files and folders that match your input. This is especially helpful for finding items quickly without completing your search.

3. **Global Search Scope**: The search bar looks across your entire account, including shared folders and files that others have made accessible to you.

Steps to Perform a Basic Search

1. **Navigate to the Search Bar**: Open the Dropbox app or web version and locate the search bar at the top.

2. **Enter a Search Query**: Start typing the name or keyword associated with your file.

3. **Review the Results**: The search results will appear in a dropdown list as you type. Select the desired file or folder from the list or press Enter to see all matching results.

4. **Refine Your Search**: If you don't find what you're looking for, try refining your search by adding more specific keywords.

Tips for Effective Searching

1. **Be Specific with Keywords**: Using specific names, dates, or phrases related to your file can help narrow down the results. For instance, instead of typing "report," use "Sales Report Q3 2024."

2. **Leverage Filters**: Dropbox allows you to apply filters like file type, date modified, and folder location. This is particularly useful for accounts with a large number of files.

3. **Search Within Folders**: If you know the general location of your file, navigate to the folder first and then use the search bar to limit the scope of your search.

4. **Capitalize on Auto-Suggestions**: Pay attention to the dropdown suggestions while typing. They often lead you directly to the file you need without completing the full search.

Advanced Search Features

For those with premium Dropbox accounts, advanced search capabilities include:

1. **Full-Text Search**: This feature scans the content within files, including PDFs and Microsoft Office documents, enabling you to search based on the text inside the document rather than just the file name.

2. **Shared File Search**: Easily locate files and folders shared with you, even if they're buried under layers of other shared items.

3. **Image Recognition**: Dropbox's AI-powered search can identify objects, locations, and text within images, making it easier to locate visuals based on content.

Troubleshooting Search Issues

Sometimes, searches may not yield the expected results. Here are a few troubleshooting tips:

1. **Ensure Proper Indexing**: Newly uploaded files may take a few moments to be indexed. If a file doesn't appear in search results, wait a few minutes and try again.

2. **Check Account Permissions**: Files shared with you might not show up if access permissions have changed. Verify with the file owner.

3. **Update Your App**: Outdated versions of the Dropbox app may not support the latest search features. Ensure you're using the latest version.

4. **Verify File Sync Status**: Files that haven't synced properly won't appear in the search results. Check your sync status and resolve any syncing issues.

Real-Life Scenarios

1. **Finding Meeting Notes**: Suppose you attended a team meeting and need the shared notes. Typing "Team Meeting Notes" in the search bar will display relevant files. Use filters like "last modified" to narrow down recent notes.

2. **Retrieving an Old Presentation**: For a presentation you created last year, enter keywords like "Marketing Presentation" and apply a date filter to locate it quickly.

3. **Searching for Shared Files**: If a colleague shared a folder called "Project X," typing "Project X" will bring it up instantly, even if it's buried among your other files.

Key Takeaways

- The search bar is a powerful tool for quick file retrieval, saving time and effort.

- Utilize advanced features like full-text search and filters to locate files more efficiently.

- Regularly update and organize your files to complement the search functionality and ensure optimal results.

In the next section, **2.3.2 Filtering Results**, we'll explore how to refine search queries further using filters for file types, dates, and locations.

2.3.2 Filtering Results

Filtering results in Dropbox is a powerful feature that helps users locate specific files or folders quickly, especially when dealing with large volumes of data. By applying filters, you can narrow down your search based on criteria such as file type, modification date, or the person who shared the file. This section will guide you through understanding and mastering Dropbox's filtering capabilities.

Understanding Filters in Dropbox

Filters act like a sieve, allowing you to exclude irrelevant data while focusing on what's important. When searching for a file, you might not always remember the exact name but may recall some attributes, like the type of file (e.g., PDF or image), when it was last edited, or the person who uploaded it. Filters leverage this partial information to refine your search.

Dropbox offers several filter categories, including:

- **File Type:** Narrow your search to documents, images, videos, or other specific types.

- **Modification Date:** Locate files based on when they were last updated.

- **Shared Status:** Identify files that are shared versus private.

- **Owner or Collaborator:** Find files by the person who created, uploaded, or shared them.

How to Apply Filters in Dropbox

Applying filters is intuitive and works similarly across the web, desktop, and mobile platforms. Here's how to use them effectively:

On the Web Interface

1. **Initiating a Search:**

   Begin by typing a keyword or phrase into the search bar at the top of the Dropbox homepage.

2. **Applying Filters:**

   - Once the search results appear, locate the filter options usually displayed on the left-hand panel or above the results.
   - Click on a filter category (e.g., **File Type**) and select the desired option, such as "PDF," "Image," or "Spreadsheet."
   - You can add multiple filters for more precise results, such as combining file type with a date range.

3. **Using Advanced Filters:**

   - For highly specific searches, use advanced filters available under the "More Filters" option.
   - Examples include filtering by starred files or files marked as "offline."

4. **Viewing Results:**

   - The filtered results will refresh automatically as you select criteria.
   - Review the refined list and select the file or folder you need.

On the Mobile App

1. **Starting Your Search:**

   Tap the search icon (magnifying glass) located in the app's navigation bar.

2. **Selecting Filters:**

- After entering a keyword, tap on the "Filters" button beneath the search bar.
- Choose from categories like file type, date, or starred items.

3. **Refining Mobile Searches:**
   - Use additional options like sorting by "Recently Opened" or "Shared With Me."
   - Mobile filters may also include quick access to offline files for easy retrieval.

4. **Accessing Results:**

Once the filter is applied, only relevant files will appear in the results list.

On the Desktop Application

1. **Searching Locally:**

The Dropbox desktop app integrates seamlessly with your operating system's search functionality. Use the search bar located within the app to begin.

2. **Filtering Results:**
   - Although filters are more limited in the desktop app, you can still refine searches by sorting files by modification date or viewing shared versus private files.
   - Use the "Recents" tab to quickly access recently modified or opened files.

Best Practices for Filtering

1. **Combine Multiple Filters:**
   - Use a combination of filters to refine your search. For example, search for "PDFs modified in the last 7 days."
   - Combining filters can save time and increase accuracy, especially in shared folders with numerous files.

2. **Leverage Starred Files:**

- If you frequently access certain files, mark them as starred.
- When searching, you can filter results to only show starred files, making them easy to find.

3. **Be Specific with Keywords:**
   - Use descriptive keywords to narrow down results before applying filters. For instance, search for "Quarterly Report" rather than "Report."

4. **Use Date Ranges Effectively:**
   - When applying a date filter, try to narrow the range as much as possible to avoid pulling in unnecessary results.

5. **Regularly Clean Up Shared Files:**
   - Keep shared folders organized to make filtering more effective.
   - Archive or remove outdated files to reduce clutter and improve search efficiency.

Advanced Filtering Techniques

Dropbox also offers some advanced features that enhance the filtering process:

1. **Search Operators:**
   - Use search operators like type:PDF or modified:today to input filters directly into the search bar.
   - This technique is especially useful for users who prefer keyboard shortcuts over mouse navigation.

2. **Integration with Third-Party Tools:**
   - When integrated with tools like Slack or Trello, Dropbox allows you to search files across platforms.
   - For example, filter results to show only files linked to a specific project or conversation.

3. **Using Tags and Metadata:**

- While Dropbox does not natively support tags, third-party apps can add metadata to files.
- This additional layer of information can make filtering more dynamic and customized.

4. **Custom Scripts for Business Accounts:**
   - For enterprise users, Dropbox offers API access to create custom scripts for advanced file organization and filtering.

Troubleshooting Filtering Issues

Sometimes, filters may not work as expected. Here's how to resolve common problems:

1. **Search Results Too Broad:**
   - Double-check the keywords and filters you've applied.
   - Ensure there are no typos or ambiguous terms in your search.

2. **Filters Not Applying:**
   - Clear your browser cache or app data if filters aren't functioning.
   - Update your Dropbox app to the latest version.

3. **Missing Files in Results:**
   - Verify that the file is not stored in an archive or another account.
   - Use the "Show Hidden Files" option if available.

4. **Contact Support:**
   - If filtering issues persist, reach out to Dropbox support for assistance.

Conclusion

Filtering results in Dropbox is an invaluable tool for managing and retrieving files efficiently. By understanding how to use filters and applying best practices, you can save time, reduce frustration, and maintain better organization across your digital workspace.

Whether you are a casual user or a professional managing extensive data, mastering filtering techniques will elevate your Dropbox experience.

2.3.3 Recent and Starred Files

Managing and quickly accessing files is a key feature of Dropbox, and the **Recent** and **Starred** sections are designed to make this task effortless. These tools allow you to save time by focusing on frequently used files or those you've interacted with most recently. This section will guide you on how to leverage these features effectively.

Understanding Recent Files

The **Recent** section in Dropbox displays files and folders that you have recently opened, edited, or uploaded. This feature is particularly useful when you're working on multiple projects and need to switch between documents without navigating through folders repeatedly.

Where to Find Recent Files

1. **Desktop App**: On the desktop interface, the Recent tab is available in the sidebar.

2. **Mobile App**: On the mobile app, tap on the **Home** tab, and you'll find the Recent files section near the top.

3. **Web Interface**: Log in to Dropbox through your browser and locate the Recent tab in the left-hand menu.

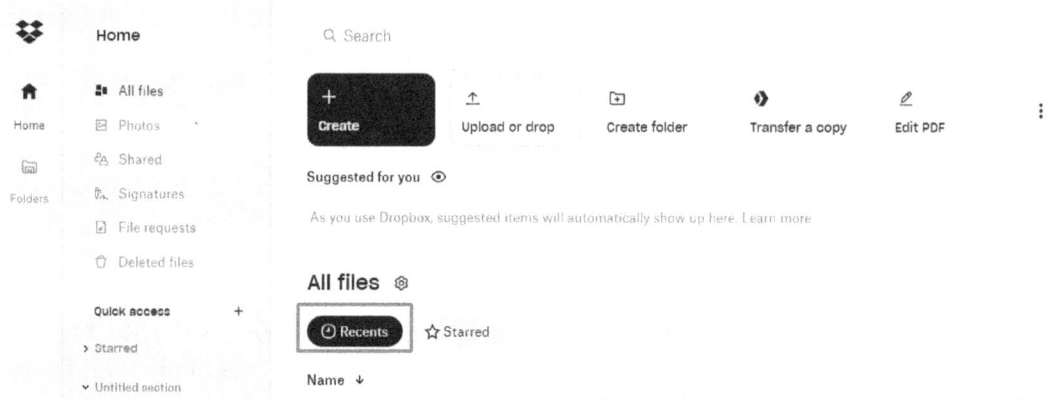

Use Cases for Recent Files

- **Ongoing Projects**: If you're working on a presentation or report, the Recent tab provides a shortcut to access your files quickly.
- **Team Collaboration**: When teammates update shared files, these changes often appear in your Recent list, making it easy to stay in sync.
- **Error Recovery**: Accidentally closed a file without saving its location? Chances are, it's in your Recent tab.

Customizing the Recent View

Unfortunately, the Recent section doesn't allow much customization, but you can optimize its usage:

- **Clear Cache Regularly**: If older files clutter your Recent list, consider manually navigating to other tabs to find what you need.
- **Rely on File Names**: Ensure your file naming conventions are clear and descriptive to locate items faster.

What Are Starred Files?

The **Starred** feature in Dropbox allows you to mark specific files or folders as favorites for quick access. Think of it as bookmarking items you need to revisit frequently. Unlike the Recent section, which updates dynamically, the Starred list is entirely under your control.

How to Star Files and Folders

Marking items as starred is a simple process:

1. **On Desktop**:
   - Right-click on the file or folder you want to star.
   - Select **Star** from the context menu.

2. **On Mobile**:
   - Tap the three-dot menu next to the file or folder.
   - Choose **Star**.

3. **On the Web**:
   - Hover over the file or folder, click on the three-dot menu, and select **Star**.

You'll notice a small star icon next to the file or folder once it's been added to your Starred list.

Accessing Starred Files

The Starred section is available on all Dropbox platforms:

- On the **desktop app**, it's a tab in the left-hand menu.
- On the **mobile app**, tap on **Home**, then scroll to find Starred items.
- On the **web interface**, click on **Starred** from the sidebar.

Why Use Starred Files?

- **Frequent Access**: Starred files are perfect for files you use daily, such as a project roadmap or frequently updated spreadsheets.
- **Priority Management**: Use the Starred list to prioritize files needing immediate attention.
- **Shared Items**: If certain shared files require frequent reference, starring them ensures they're always accessible.

Tips for Maximizing Recent and Starred Features

1. Combine Recent and Starred Features

While Recent is automated and Starred is manual, the two can work in tandem. For example:

- Use **Recent** for dynamic workflows where files frequently change.
- Use **Starred** to pin files that are critical over a longer period, such as client contracts or a quarterly report template.

2. Periodically Update Your Starred List

To avoid clutter, review your Starred list periodically:

- Remove files that are no longer relevant.
- Add new files that have become essential to your current work.

3. Leverage Starred for Mobile Productivity

On the mobile app, the Starred list acts as a shortcut when working on the go. Use it to minimize navigation time during meetings or while traveling.

4. Utilize Naming Conventions for Better Sorting

Files in both Recent and Starred sections are displayed by name. Clear and concise file naming conventions can make it easier to identify files at a glance. For example, prefix your files with project codes or dates (e.g., "2024_Q1_Report" or "ClientA_Proposal").

5. Sync Across Devices

Both Recent and Starred features are synced across all devices linked to your Dropbox account. This means changes you make on one device will be reflected on others, ensuring consistency and ease of use.

Common Pitfalls and How to Avoid Them

Overloading Your Starred List

While it's tempting to star many files, an overloaded list defeats its purpose. To maintain efficiency:

- Stick to 10–15 starred items at a time.

- Use folders instead of individual files when applicable.

Misinterpreting the Recent List

Recent files don't always represent the most important files—they simply reflect the latest activity. To avoid confusion, rely on the Starred feature for essential files.

Ignoring Regular Maintenance

Neglecting to update your Starred list or clear outdated files from Recent can lead to clutter. Set a reminder to tidy up these sections monthly.

The Power of Recent and Starred for Team Collaboration

When working in teams, both Recent and Starred become even more valuable:

- **Shared Activity Tracking**: The Recent tab lets you monitor changes made by others in shared folders.

- **Starred for Team Projects**: Encourage team members to star shared files, ensuring everyone knows where to find critical documents.

By mastering the **Recent** and **Starred** features, you can streamline your workflow, reduce time spent searching for files, and stay organized across all your devices. These tools, though simple, form the foundation of efficient file management in Dropbox.

CHAPTER III
Sharing and Collaboration

3.1 Sharing Files and Folders

3.1.1 Sharing Links

Sharing links is one of Dropbox's most powerful and user-friendly features, enabling users to distribute files or folders without worrying about attachment size limits or platform compatibility. Whether you're sharing photos with friends, project files with colleagues, or large documents with clients, Dropbox makes the process seamless and secure. In this section, we'll cover how to create and customize sharing links, manage permissions, and optimize link sharing for various use cases.

1. Understanding Dropbox Sharing Links

Dropbox sharing links are unique URLs that provide access to specific files or folders stored in your account. They're designed to make file sharing convenient, removing the need for recipients to have a Dropbox account. Once a link is created, you can share it via email, messaging apps, or social media.

Key Benefits of Sharing Links:

- **No Account Needed:** Recipients can view or download files without signing up for Dropbox.

- **Large File Support:** Share files much larger than traditional email attachment limits.

- **Customizable Permissions:** Control what recipients can do with the shared file—view only, download, or edit.

2. How to Create a Sharing Link

Creating a sharing link in Dropbox is straightforward and can be done through various platforms—desktop, mobile, or web. Below are step-by-step instructions for each platform:

On the Web Interface:

1. **Log in to Dropbox:** Navigate to Dropbox.com and sign in.
2. **Locate the File/Folder:** Find the item you want to share.
3. **Click 'Share':** Hover over the file or folder, and click the blue "Share" button.
4. **Generate Link:** In the sharing window, click "Create a link." Dropbox will automatically generate a unique URL.
5. **Copy and Share:** Click "Copy Link" and paste it into your preferred communication platform.

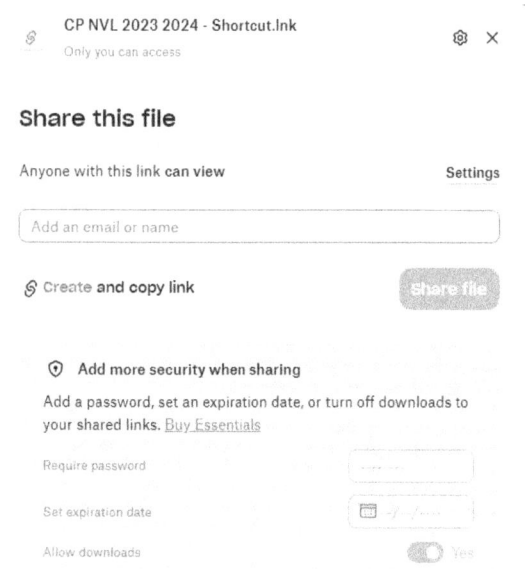

On the Desktop App:

1. **Open the Dropbox Folder:** Navigate to the Dropbox folder on your computer.
2. **Right-Click the Item:** Select the file or folder, right-click, and choose "Share" or "Copy Dropbox Link."
3. **Share the Link:** The link is copied to your clipboard. Paste it wherever needed.

On the Mobile App:

1. **Open the Dropbox App:** Launch the Dropbox app on your smartphone or tablet.
2. **Find the Item:** Navigate to the file or folder.
3. **Tap the '…' Icon:** Next to the item, tap the three-dot menu, then select "Share."
4. **Create the Link:** Tap "Create a link."
5. **Distribute the Link:** Share it via messaging apps, email, or social media.

3. Customizing Sharing Links

Once a link is created, Dropbox allows you to customize its settings to suit your specific needs.

Adjusting Permissions:

- **View-Only Access:** By default, recipients can only view and download files.
- **Edit Access (Dropbox Accounts Only):** If you want recipients to collaborate, enable editing rights. This option requires the recipient to have a Dropbox account.

Setting Expiration Dates (Professional Plans):

If you're on a Dropbox Professional or Business plan, you can set expiration dates for links, ensuring they remain accessible only for a specific period.

Adding Password Protection:

For added security, you can password-protect your sharing links. This ensures only users with the correct password can access the file or folder.

4. Managing Shared Links

Dropbox provides a dashboard where you can monitor and manage all your shared links.

Viewing Active Links:

1. **Access the Dashboard:** Go to the "Shared" tab in the web or mobile app.
2. **Review Links:** See a list of files and folders with active links.

Revoking Access:

If you no longer want a link to be active, you can revoke it:

1. **Locate the Link:** Find the shared file or folder in your Dropbox.
2. **Click 'Share':** Open the sharing settings.
3. **Remove the Link:** Click "Delete link" to disable it.

Tracking Link Activity (Advanced Plans):

On higher-tier plans, Dropbox provides analytics for shared links. You can track:

- **Views:** How many times the file or folder was accessed.
- **Downloads:** The number of times the file was downloaded.
- **Who Accessed:** If shared with named users, you can see who interacted with the link.

5. Best Practices for Sharing Links

To maximize the effectiveness of Dropbox sharing links, consider these tips:

Organize Your Files:

Ensure files are well-organized and properly named before sharing. This makes it easier for recipients to navigate.

Use Descriptive Links:

Add context when sharing links. Instead of just pasting a URL, include a message explaining what the link contains.

Secure Sensitive Information:

For confidential files, always use password protection and expiration dates. Avoid sharing sensitive information over unsecured platforms.

Regularly Audit Shared Links:

Periodically review your active links to ensure only necessary files remain accessible.

6. Use Cases for Sharing Links

Sharing links is versatile and can be applied in various scenarios:

Personal Use:

- Sharing vacation photos with family.
- Sending large video files to friends.

Professional Use:

- Distributing project documents to a team.

- Sharing portfolios or resumes with potential clients.

Educational Use:

- Providing access to class materials.
- Sharing research papers or collaborative projects.

Conclusion

Mastering the art of sharing links in Dropbox can significantly enhance your file-sharing capabilities. By leveraging Dropbox's robust sharing tools, you can ensure your files are accessible, secure, and easy to manage. In the next section, we'll explore how to set permissions for shared files, enabling you to maintain control over your digital content.

3.1.2 Setting Permissions for Shared Files

When sharing files and folders in Dropbox, setting appropriate permissions is a crucial step to ensure that your content is used as intended while maintaining security and control. Permissions determine who can view, edit, or share the files you've uploaded to Dropbox. Understanding how to configure these permissions effectively will help you collaborate more securely and efficiently.

Understanding Permission Levels

Dropbox offers three primary permission levels:

1. **Viewer Access**: This is the most restrictive access level, allowing recipients only to view or download files. They cannot make changes or add comments unless granted additional permissions. Viewer access is ideal for sharing files that need to be reviewed but not altered.

2. **Editor Access**: This level allows recipients to view, edit, add, delete, and comment on files. Editor access is suitable for collaborative projects where multiple users are actively contributing.

3. **Owner Access**: As the original uploader, you maintain ownership of the file or folder. Owners have complete control over sharing permissions and can transfer ownership if needed.

How to Set Permissions for Files and Folders

1. Sharing Files with Custom Permissions

To share a file and set permissions:

1. Locate the file you want to share in Dropbox.
2. Right-click (or long-press on mobile) and select **"Share"**.
3. Enter the email address or name of the person you want to share the file with.
4. Use the dropdown menu next to their name to select the permission level: **Viewer** or **Editor**.
5. Click **"Share"** to send the invitation.

2. Sharing Folders with Custom Permissions

When sharing a folder, permissions apply to all files within that folder. This is useful for team projects or shared resources. To share a folder:

1. Right-click the folder and select **"Share"**.
2. Add the recipients by entering their email addresses.
3. Assign permissions (Viewer or Editor) to each recipient.
4. If you want recipients to add files but not edit existing ones, select **"Can view and add"**.

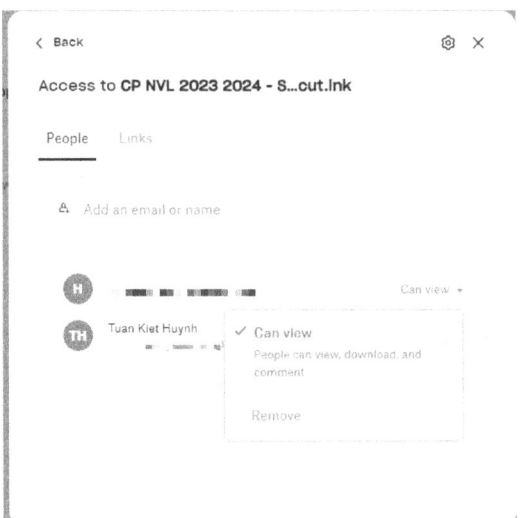

3. Adjusting Permissions on Existing Shares

You can modify permissions at any time:

1. Go to the file or folder's **Shared** settings.
2. Find the recipient's name under **Who can access**.
3. Use the dropdown menu next to their name to adjust permissions or remove their access.

Advanced Permission Settings

Dropbox offers additional controls to refine how files are shared:

1. Setting Expiry Dates for Links

For sensitive documents, you can set a link to expire after a specific period:

1. When generating a shareable link, click **"Settings"**.
2. Enable the **"Link expires"** option and set the desired expiration date.
3. Share the link as usual, knowing it will no longer work after the set date.

2. Adding Password Protection

Protect your shared links with a password to prevent unauthorized access:

1. Open the **"Settings"** menu while creating the link.
2. Enable **"Password protect"** and set a secure password.
3. Share both the link and password with your intended recipient.

3. Disabling Downloads

If you don't want recipients to download the file, you can restrict this option:

1. In the share settings, toggle **"Disable downloads"**.
2. Recipients will still be able to view the file online but won't be able to save it locally.

Practical Scenarios for Permission Settings

Scenario 1: Sharing a Proposal with a Client

When sending a proposal, you may only want the client to view the file without the ability to edit or share it. Set their permission to **Viewer**, and add password protection for extra security.

Scenario 2: Collaborating on a Team Project

For a team project, grant **Editor** access to team members who need to make changes. Assign **Viewer** access to stakeholders who only need to review progress.

Scenario 3: Sharing a Folder with Mixed Permissions

For a shared folder containing various documents:

- Assign **Editor** access to team members working on editable files.
- Assign **Viewer** access to external collaborators who only need to review completed work.

Best Practices for Managing Permissions

1. **Grant the Minimum Required Access**: Always give recipients the least amount of access they need. This reduces the risk of accidental changes or data breaches.

2. **Review Permissions Regularly**: Periodically check who has access to your files and folders to ensure permissions are still relevant.

3. **Use Team Folders for Collaborative Projects**: For teams, consider using Dropbox Business with team folders to manage access more efficiently.

4. **Monitor Activity Logs**: Keep track of who is viewing or editing your files. Dropbox provides an activity log for each shared item to help you stay informed.

Troubleshooting Permission Issues

If you encounter issues with sharing permissions:

- **Recipient Can't Access File**: Double-check their email address and ensure the link is still active.

- **Changes Not Visible**: Ensure that collaborators have **Editor** access and are syncing the latest version.

- **Unauthorized Changes**: Use version history to restore the original file and adjust permissions to prevent further edits.

By mastering Dropbox's permission settings, you can share files securely and collaborate effectively while maintaining control over your data. These tools provide flexibility and precision, empowering users to tailor their sharing experience to any situation.

3.1.3 Managing Shared Folders

Shared folders are one of Dropbox's most powerful tools, designed to facilitate seamless collaboration among individuals and teams. Whether you're coordinating a project, sharing files with a client, or collaborating on documents with classmates, managing shared folders effectively ensures smooth workflows and avoids potential confusion. This section dives into the essential practices, tools, and tips for managing shared folders in Dropbox.

Understanding Shared Folders in Dropbox

Shared folders allow multiple users to access, edit, and manage the files within a specific folder. When you create a shared folder, you control who has access, their level of permissions, and the updates they can make. Here's a breakdown of how shared folders function:

- **Shared Space**: All members can view the folder in their Dropbox accounts, ensuring everyone works on the same set of files.

- **Real-Time Syncing**: Any changes made by one member, such as edits, deletions, or file additions, are automatically synced across all members' devices.

- **Permission Settings**: You can assign specific roles to collaborators, such as allowing them to only view files or granting them the ability to edit and reorganize content.

Creating and Sharing a Folder

To share a folder, simply right-click or use the options menu within Dropbox, select "Share," and invite collaborators by entering their email addresses. From here, managing a shared folder becomes critical to ensure its proper use and security.

Managing Permissions in Shared Folders

Dropbox provides fine-tuned control over permissions in shared folders. This flexibility helps ensure that collaborators can only access the files they need and can perform actions appropriate to their roles.

1. **Editing Permissions**

    - **Editor Role**: Collaborators with editing permissions can add, delete, and modify files within the folder. Use this setting for team members actively working on projects.

    - **Viewer Role**: Collaborators with view-only access can see and download files but cannot make changes. This is ideal for stakeholders or external parties who only need to review content.

    - **How to Change Permissions**:

        1. Right-click on the shared folder.

2. Select "Share" and locate the collaborator's name.

3. Use the dropdown menu next to their name to select the appropriate permission level.

2. **Revoking Access**

    If someone no longer needs access to a shared folder, you can easily remove them:

    - Go to the "Sharing" settings of the folder.
    - Locate the person's name in the list of collaborators.
    - Click the "Remove" or "X" button next to their name.

3. **Managing Group Access**

    Dropbox allows you to share folders with groups instead of individuals. This feature simplifies management when collaborating with teams. Adjusting group permissions automatically applies changes to all members of the group.

Tracking Changes and Activity in Shared Folders

Transparency is crucial when managing shared folders. Dropbox provides tools to track changes and ensure everyone stays informed.

1. **Viewing Activity Logs**

    Activity logs display a detailed history of changes made within a shared folder. You can see:

    - Files added or deleted.
    - Edits made by specific users.
    - Changes in permissions.

    To access the activity log:

    - Navigate to the folder in the Dropbox interface.
    - Click on the "Activity" tab to view the history.

2. **Using Notifications**

Dropbox notifications alert you to changes in shared folders. These updates help you stay informed without constantly checking the folder.

- o   Enable notifications in your Dropbox app settings.
- o   Customize the types of notifications you want to receive, such as edits, file uploads, or permission changes.

Organizing Shared Folders for Clarity

Effective organization prevents shared folders from becoming cluttered and confusing. Here are some best practices:

1. **Naming Conventions**

   Use clear, descriptive names for shared folders. For example, instead of "Project," use "Client ABC - Marketing Campaign."

2. **Subfolders**
   Break down large projects into subfolders to organize files by category or phase. For example:
   - o   "Phase 1: Research"
   - o   "Phase 2: Design"
   - o   "Phase 3: Final Delivery"

3. **Archiving Completed Projects**

   Move completed projects to an archive folder to declutter your active workspace while keeping older files accessible.

Resolving Conflicts in Shared Folders

File conflicts can occur when multiple users edit a file simultaneously or if someone uploads a file with the same name as an existing one. Dropbox helps you resolve these conflicts efficiently:

1. **File Versioning**

Dropbox retains multiple versions of a file, so you can compare edits and restore an earlier version if needed.

- Locate the file in question.
- Right-click and select "Version history."
- Choose the version you want to restore or download for review.

2. **Renaming Conflicting Files**

Dropbox automatically renames conflicting files to avoid overwriting. Review both files, determine the correct one, and delete or rename the unnecessary version.

Tips for Managing Shared Folders in Teams

For teams, shared folders become even more critical. Here are strategies to maximize efficiency:

1. **Regular Folder Audits**

Periodically review the shared folder's contents to remove outdated files and ensure only relevant materials remain.

2. **Setting Clear Expectations**

Communicate folder usage guidelines to collaborators. For example, specify:

- Naming conventions.
- Folder structure.
- Who is responsible for maintaining the folder.

3. **Using Dropbox Paper for Coordination**

Dropbox Paper, integrated with shared folders, allows teams to document guidelines, updates, or notes related to the folder.

Conclusion

Managing shared folders effectively is essential for collaboration success. By understanding permission settings, tracking changes, and organizing files systematically, you can ensure that everyone works efficiently and securely. Whether for personal use or team projects, mastering these skills will elevate your Dropbox experience.

3.2 Collaborating with Others

3.2.1 Real-Time Editing with Dropbox Paper

Collaboration is a cornerstone of productivity in today's interconnected world. Dropbox Paper, a powerful tool integrated into the Dropbox ecosystem, takes collaboration to the next level by enabling real-time editing and co-authoring of documents. Whether you're working on a brainstorming session, a project proposal, or team notes, Dropbox Paper ensures seamless teamwork in a unified, user-friendly environment.

What is Dropbox Paper?

Dropbox Paper is a collaborative document-editing tool that combines simplicity with powerful features. Unlike traditional word processors, Dropbox Paper emphasizes real-time collaboration and creativity. Multiple users can simultaneously edit a document, comment on specific sections, and share ideas—all within the same interface.

Dropbox Paper is particularly suited for:

- Team brainstorming sessions
- Project management documentation
- Collaborative reports and meeting notes
- Creative content creation and editing

Setting Up Your Dropbox Paper Document

Creating a new Dropbox Paper document is straightforward:

1. Log in to your Dropbox account.
2. Click on the **"Paper"** option in the left navigation bar.
3. Select **"Create a New Doc"** to start with a blank document.

You can also access templates for meeting agendas, project timelines, and more, which save time and provide structured formats for specific tasks.

Real-Time Collaboration in Action

Dropbox Paper allows users to collaborate in real time, meaning that changes made by one user are instantly visible to all participants. Here's how this feature stands out:

- **Simultaneous Editing:** Multiple users can work on the same document at once. Changes are color-coded or tagged with the editor's name, allowing easy identification of contributors.

- **Comment Threads:** Team members can add comments to specific lines, paragraphs, or even images. These comments can include tags (e.g., @username) to notify specific individuals, ensuring questions and feedback are directed to the right person.

- **Inline Annotations:** For precise feedback, users can highlight text or content and leave contextual notes without disrupting the document's flow.

Features That Enhance Real-Time Collaboration

Dropbox Paper includes several features tailored to improve real-time collaboration:

1. **Task Assignment and Tracking:**
    - Assign tasks directly within the document by tagging team members with @username.
    - Add checkboxes to track progress on specific tasks.
    - Create to-do lists that integrate with due dates and notifications, ensuring accountability.

2. **Rich Media Embedding:**
    - Insert images, videos, GIFs, or even web links into the document to enrich content.
    - Drag-and-drop functionality allows seamless media integration, making documents visually appealing and interactive.

3. **Templates for Structured Collaboration:**
    - Use pre-built templates for specific needs, such as meeting agendas, project timelines, or design feedback sessions.
    - Custom templates can be created to fit your team's unique workflows.

4. **Version History:**

- Access the document's version history to track changes made by collaborators.
- Restore previous versions if necessary, preventing accidental loss of critical information.

Best Practices for Effective Collaboration

To maximize productivity and minimize confusion during real-time editing, follow these best practices:

- **Set Ground Rules:** Establish clear guidelines for editing, such as who is responsible for specific sections or tasks.
- **Use Comments Wisely:** Instead of overwriting someone else's work, use comments to suggest edits or improvements.
- **Designate a Lead Editor:** Assign one person as the document owner or lead editor to oversee final revisions and ensure consistency.
- **Communicate Expectations:** Before starting, clarify the document's purpose and deadlines to keep the team aligned.

Advantages of Real-Time Editing with Dropbox Paper

Dropbox Paper's real-time editing capabilities provide numerous benefits to teams, including:

1. **Increased Efficiency:**

   Real-time collaboration eliminates the need for back-and-forth emails or waiting for someone to finish their edits. Everyone works together on the same platform, saving time.

2. **Enhanced Creativity:**

   The collaborative environment fosters creativity by encouraging instant feedback and brainstorming. Team members can build on each other's ideas without delay.

3. **Transparency and Accountability:**

   Changes are tracked with timestamps and contributor names, ensuring transparency and accountability.

4. **Ease of Use:**

Dropbox Paper's minimalist interface makes it easy for everyone, regardless of technical expertise, to participate effectively.

Use Cases for Dropbox Paper in Collaboration

Real-time editing with Dropbox Paper is invaluable for many scenarios:

- **Team Brainstorms:** Use a blank document as a digital whiteboard, allowing team members to jot down ideas simultaneously.

- **Meeting Notes:** Collaboratively take meeting notes that everyone can access and update in real-time.

- **Content Creation:** Teams can draft, revise, and finalize blog posts, reports, or presentations together.

- **Project Timelines:** Create and adjust project timelines on the fly, keeping everyone updated on responsibilities and deadlines.

Integrating Dropbox Paper with Other Tools

Dropbox Paper integrates seamlessly with other tools to enhance collaboration:

- **Dropbox Files:** Embed Dropbox files directly into Paper documents, making them accessible for reference or editing.

- **Calendar Integration:** Sync Dropbox Paper documents with Google Calendar or Outlook for streamlined meeting agendas.

- **Third-Party Apps:** Incorporate links from tools like Trello, Slack, or Asana to centralize information within the Paper document.

Common Challenges and How to Overcome Them

Despite its powerful features, some users may face challenges:

1. **Too Many Contributors:** If too many people edit simultaneously, the document can become cluttered. Solution: Assign roles or restrict editing permissions as needed.

2. **Miscommunication:** Misunderstandings about tasks can arise. Solution: Use comments and task assignment features to clarify responsibilities.

3. **Technical Glitches:** Occasionally, connectivity issues may disrupt real-time updates. Solution: Ensure a stable internet connection and save work frequently.

Final Thoughts on Real-Time Collaboration

Dropbox Paper is a game-changer for real-time collaboration, offering teams an intuitive and efficient way to work together. By leveraging its robust features and adopting best practices, you can streamline workflows, enhance communication, and achieve better results in less time.

Whether you're collaborating across departments or working on a group project, Dropbox Paper ensures that your team's efforts are synchronized, productive, and impactful.

3.2.2 Commenting on Files

Dropbox is not just a file storage and sharing platform; it is also a collaborative workspace where teams can communicate effectively without switching between multiple tools. One of its most useful features for collaboration is **commenting on files**. This feature allows team members to provide feedback, suggest edits, and ask questions directly on the files stored in Dropbox, making communication clear and contextual. In this section, we'll explore the ins and outs of commenting on files in Dropbox, including its advantages, how to use it effectively, and best practices for teams.

Why Use Comments on Dropbox Files?

The ability to comment on files offers several advantages, particularly for teams working in distributed or remote environments:

1. **Centralized Communication**:

    Comments are tied directly to the specific file being discussed. This eliminates the confusion of tracking feedback across email chains or other communication platforms.

2. **Improved Context**:

    Comments allow users to refer to specific sections of a file, providing precise feedback. For instance, on a document, you can highlight text or a paragraph to make your comment more relevant.

3. **Real-Time Updates**:

   Team members are notified when comments are added, ensuring everyone stays updated with the latest feedback.

4. **Time-Saving**:
   By integrating discussions into the file itself, Dropbox reduces the time spent on back-and-forth exchanges across separate tools.

How to Add Comments to Files in Dropbox

1. Adding General Comments

- Open a file in the Dropbox preview mode (this works for documents, PDFs, images, and videos).

- Look for the comment icon (usually a speech bubble) on the right-hand side of the interface.

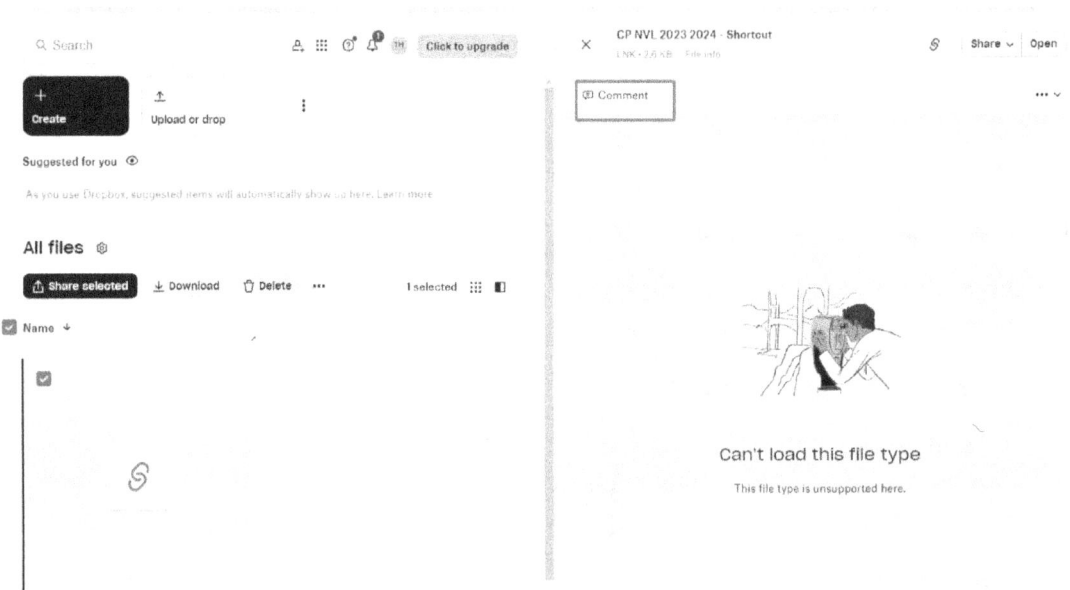

- Type your comment in the text box provided and click **Post**.

CHAPTER III: SHARING AND COLLABORATION

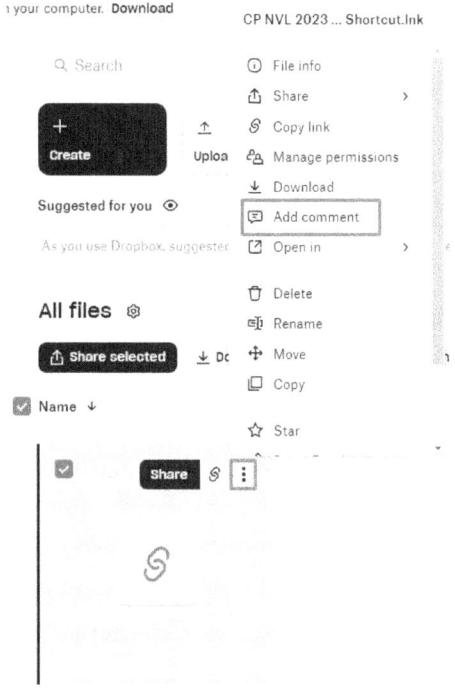

2. Adding Specific Comments

- For documents or images, you can highlight specific sections or select a specific area where your comment applies.
- Click on the selected area to open the comment box and add your feedback.

3. Replying to Comments

- When a comment is posted, other collaborators can reply directly beneath it. This threaded conversation style keeps discussions organized and easy to follow.

4. Resolving Comments

- Once a comment has been addressed, you can mark it as resolved. This helps keep the file clean and ensures that unresolved feedback remains visible.

Best Practices for Commenting on Dropbox Files

To maximize the value of Dropbox's commenting feature, it's essential to follow a few best practices:

1. **Be Specific**:

   Avoid vague feedback like "This needs improvement." Instead, provide actionable suggestions, such as "Consider rephrasing this sentence to make it more concise."

2. **Use Mentions**:

   Tag team members by typing **@username** to ensure they are notified of your comment. For example, "@JohnDoe, could you clarify this section?"

3. **Keep Comments Concise**:

   Lengthy comments can be overwhelming. Stick to clear and direct points to keep the feedback process efficient.

4. **Stay Professional**:

   Maintain a respectful tone in all comments, even when providing constructive criticism.

5. **Resolve When Done**:

   Mark comments as resolved once the issue has been addressed to keep the workspace clutter-free.

Examples of Effective Commenting Scenarios

Scenario 1: Editing a Marketing Proposal

Imagine your team is reviewing a marketing proposal uploaded to Dropbox. One team member highlights a section about the target audience and comments, "@MarketingLead, should we include additional data on audience demographics here?" Another member adds a reply beneath it, "Good idea! I'll pull the stats from last quarter's report."

Scenario 2: Reviewing a Design Mockup

Your design team uploads a website mockup. A collaborator clicks on the header section of the mockup and comments, "Can we try a darker shade of blue here? It might stand out more." Another teammate responds, "Good point, I'll make the adjustment and upload a revised version shortly."

Managing and Tracking Comments

Dropbox makes it easy to manage and track comments across multiple files:

1. **Notifications**:

   When someone adds or replies to a comment on a file you own or follow, you'll receive a notification in Dropbox and via email (if enabled).

2. **Activity Logs**:

   The activity log for each file shows all recent changes, including new comments, edits, and resolutions.

3. **Filtering Comments**:

   You can filter comments by status (e.g., unresolved or resolved) or by user to focus on specific discussions.

4. **Exporting Comments**:

   For certain file types, Dropbox allows you to export comments as part of a review summary, making it easier to archive feedback.

Using Dropbox Paper for Advanced Commenting

Dropbox Paper, an integrated tool within Dropbox, takes collaboration a step further with real-time editing and advanced commenting features:

- **In-Line Comments**: Add comments directly next to text, images, or tables in a Paper document.
- **Emoji Reactions**: Use emoji responses for quick feedback on specific sections.
- **To-Do Lists**: Convert comments into actionable tasks by creating checkboxes directly from the feedback.

Overcoming Common Challenges in Commenting

While commenting is a straightforward feature, some challenges may arise:

1. **Overlapping Feedback**:

   Solution: Establish a review protocol to assign specific sections to individual reviewers, minimizing duplicate feedback.

2. **Miscommunication**:
   Solution: Use clear and precise language. If a comment requires clarification, follow up in a reply.

3. **Delayed Responses**:

   Solution: Set expectations for feedback timelines and use mentions to notify the relevant team members.

Conclusion

Commenting on files in Dropbox is an invaluable tool for fostering collaboration, streamlining feedback, and keeping teams aligned. By using this feature effectively and following best practices, you can enhance communication and productivity, ensuring that every project progresses smoothly. Whether you're reviewing a design, editing a document, or finalizing a presentation, Dropbox's commenting feature keeps everyone on the same page—literally and figuratively.

3.2.3 Activity Notifications and Logs

Collaboration in Dropbox isn't just about sharing files and editing documents—it's also about staying informed. Activity notifications and logs are essential tools that help users keep track of what's happening with their shared files and folders. By leveraging these features, you can ensure a transparent, efficient, and secure collaboration process. This section explores how Dropbox's activity tracking and notification system works, how to use it effectively, and tips for managing activity logs to stay on top of your projects.

Understanding Activity Notifications

Dropbox sends activity notifications to inform you about changes, updates, or interactions involving your files and folders. These notifications are designed to keep you in the loop without overwhelming you with unnecessary alerts.

Types of Activity Notifications:

1. **File Edits:** Notifications about changes to shared files, such as edits, updates, or renames.

2. **Comments:** Alerts when someone adds, replies to, or resolves a comment on your file.

3. **Shares and Access Changes:** Notifications when a file or folder is shared, or when permissions are updated.

4. **Deletions:** Alerts if a file in a shared folder is deleted.

5. **Activity Summaries:** Periodic updates summarizing recent activities, available in email or through the app.

Customizing Notifications: To avoid information overload, Dropbox allows you to customize the types of notifications you receive. Here's how to adjust your preferences:

- **Mobile App:** Go to the settings menu, select **Notifications**, and toggle on or off specific activity types.

- **Desktop or Web:** Navigate to your account settings, locate the **Notifications** tab, and adjust the preferences to suit your needs.

Best Practices for Notifications:

- Limit notifications to critical changes for high-traffic folders.

- Use email notifications for major updates, while relying on app alerts for day-to-day activities.

- Regularly review your settings to ensure they align with your current collaboration needs.

Tracking Activity Logs

Activity logs are a powerful tool for understanding the history of interactions with your files and folders. They provide a detailed timeline of actions, such as uploads, edits, shares, and deletions. These logs are especially useful for auditing, troubleshooting, and maintaining accountability in collaborative projects.

Accessing the Activity Log:

- **Web Interface:** Navigate to a file or folder, click the **Activity** tab on the right-hand panel, and view a chronological list of events.

- **Mobile App:** Open a file or folder, tap the **Details** option, and scroll down to the activity section.

Information in Activity Logs:

1. **User Details:** The name or email of the user who performed the action.

2. **Action Type:** Specific actions such as viewed, edited, commented, or shared.

3. **Timestamp:** The exact time and date the action occurred.

4. **Contextual Details:** Information about changes, such as the new file name or updated permissions.

Use Cases for Activity Logs:

- **Auditing:** Ensure that team members are complying with collaboration guidelines.

- **Conflict Resolution:** Identify who made changes and when, helping to resolve disputes.

- **Security Monitoring:** Detect unauthorized access or suspicious activities.

Managing and Exporting Activity Logs

For teams or organizations, managing and exporting activity logs can provide deeper insights into file usage patterns and collaborative workflows.

Advanced Options for Teams: Dropbox Business and Advanced accounts offer additional tools for managing activity logs:

- **Admin Console:** Access detailed activity reports for all team members, including external collaborators.

- **Filters and Searches:** Use filters to narrow down logs by date, action type, or specific users.
- **Integrations:** Export logs to third-party tools like Tableau or Excel for analysis.

Steps to Export Activity Logs:

1. Open the **Admin Console** for your Dropbox Business account.
2. Go to the **Activity** section.
3. Use filters to customize the data you want to export.
4. Click the **Export** button and download the file in CSV format.

Practical Applications of Exported Logs:

- **Performance Tracking:** Analyze collaboration efficiency over time.
- **Security Audits:** Ensure compliance with organizational policies.
- **Backup Plans:** Use logs to identify critical files and users for backup strategies.

Tips for Managing Notifications and Logs Effectively

While notifications and logs are valuable, managing them efficiently is key to avoiding distractions and ensuring smooth collaboration. Here are some practical tips:

1. **Group Notifications by Priority:**

   Set up rules to differentiate high-priority alerts (e.g., changes to client deliverables) from routine updates.

2. **Schedule Time for Log Reviews:**

   Instead of checking logs in real-time, dedicate a specific time each week to review and analyze activity logs.

3. **Train Your Team:**

   Educate team members on how to use activity logs and notifications to reduce dependency on frequent manual updates.

4. **Leverage Automation:**

Integrate Dropbox logs with project management tools like Slack or Asana to automate updates and reminders.

5. **Focus on Data Privacy:**

   Regularly review who has access to sensitive activity logs and implement safeguards to protect this information.

Conclusion

Activity notifications and logs are indispensable tools for anyone using Dropbox to collaborate effectively. By understanding how to configure notifications, access activity logs, and use advanced features, you can streamline communication, enhance transparency, and boost productivity in any collaborative project. Whether you're working with a small team or managing a large organization, mastering these tools will give you greater control over your Dropbox workspace and ensure that your files are always in safe hands.

3.3 Dropbox for Teams

3.3.1 Setting Up a Team Account

Dropbox is not just a personal storage tool; it also offers robust features designed for businesses and teams. Setting up a team account allows members to collaborate more effectively, centralize file management, and maintain control over shared resources. This section will guide you through the process of creating and configuring a Dropbox team account, ensuring your team gets the most out of this powerful tool.

Step 1: Choosing the Right Plan for Your Team

Before setting up a team account, you need to decide on the Dropbox plan that suits your team's needs. Dropbox offers several business plans, each with varying features:

1. **Dropbox Standard:**
    - Ideal for smaller teams or startups.
    - Includes 5 TB of shared storage.
    - Basic collaboration and admin tools.

2. **Dropbox Advanced:**
    - Designed for growing teams with larger storage needs.
    - Unlimited storage.
    - Advanced admin, audit, and security tools.

3. **Dropbox Enterprise:**
    - Tailored for large organizations with complex workflows.
    - Customizable storage and security features.
    - Priority support and onboarding assistance.

Evaluate your team's size, storage requirements, and budget before selecting a plan. Dropbox also offers free trials, which can help you assess its suitability before committing.

Step 2: Creating the Team Account

1. **Sign Up or Upgrade:**
   - If you already have a personal Dropbox account, you can upgrade it to a business plan.
   - Visit the Dropbox Business page, choose your desired plan, and follow the prompts to set up your team account.

2. **Enter Team Information:**
   - Name your team account to reflect your organization or project name. For example, "Acme Marketing Team."
   - Add a description if needed, especially for larger organizations managing multiple teams.

3. **Invite Team Members:**
   - Enter email addresses of the team members you wish to invite.
   - Dropbox will send them an invitation to join the team account.

4. **Configure Payment Options:**
   - Input your payment details to activate the account. You can opt for monthly or annual billing.
   - Keep in mind that annual billing often comes with discounts.

Step 3: Organizing Your Team's Workspace

Once the account is created, organizing your team's workspace is crucial for effective collaboration.

1. **Creating Shared Folders:**

- Set up shared folders for different departments or projects. For example:
    - "Marketing Campaigns"
    - "Product Development"
    - "HR Policies"

2. **Assigning Folder Permissions:**
    - Define access levels for each folder:
        - **Editor:** Can view, edit, and share files.
        - **Viewer:** Can only view files.
    - Assign permissions based on team roles. For example, only HR staff should have edit access to the "HR Policies" folder.

3. **Using Team Spaces:**
    - Team Spaces are centralized areas where all team members can access shared files.
    - Add essential documents, templates, and guidelines to this space for quick access.

Step 4: Managing Team Members

Efficient team management ensures that the right people have the right access to resources.

1. **Adding or Removing Members:**
    - To add new members, go to the Admin Console, navigate to "Members," and select "Invite Members."
    - To remove a member, deactivate their access in the same section. Deactivated members lose access to team files, but their activity logs remain available.

2. **Setting Roles:**

- Assign roles like **Admin** (full control) or **Member** (limited control) based on responsibilities.
- For example, an Admin can invite members, manage billing, and monitor activity logs, while Members primarily work with files.

3. **Monitoring Activity:**
    - Use the Activity tab in the Admin Console to track file access, edits, and downloads.
    - This feature is particularly useful for identifying potential security issues or bottlenecks in workflow.

Step 5: Customizing Team Settings

Dropbox offers several customization options to tailor the platform to your team's needs.

1. **Branding Your Account:**
    - Add your company logo to shared folders and links for a professional appearance.
    - This is especially valuable for client-facing teams.
2. **Enforcing Security Policies:**
    - Enable two-factor authentication for all members.
    - Set up device approvals to restrict access to trusted devices.
3. **Configuring Notifications:**
    - Customize notification settings to avoid overload.
    - For example, team leads might want to receive updates for all shared files, while other members may only need project-specific alerts.

Step 6: Integrating Third-Party Tools

Dropbox integrates seamlessly with numerous tools to enhance productivity:

1. **Project Management Tools:**

- Integrate Dropbox with Trello or Asana to attach files directly to tasks.

2. **Collaboration Platforms:**
    - Use Slack integration to share files in team chats.

3. **Document Editing:**
    - Connect with Google Workspace or Microsoft Office for real-time document collaboration.

Step 7: Training Your Team

To maximize the potential of Dropbox, ensure all team members are well-trained:

1. **Hosting Onboarding Sessions:**
    - Conduct a walkthrough of the platform's key features.
    - Provide examples of best practices for file organization and collaboration.

2. **Sharing Tutorials and Resources:**
    - Dropbox offers a library of help articles and video tutorials. Share these resources with your team.

3. **Encouraging Feedback:**
    - Regularly gather feedback from team members about their experience with Dropbox.
    - Use this feedback to refine folder structures, permissions, and workflows.

Step 8: Scaling Up Your Dropbox Team Account

As your organization grows, your Dropbox usage will evolve.

1. **Upgrading Your Plan:**
    - If your storage needs increase, consider moving to the Advanced or Enterprise plan.

2. **Adding More Members:**

- Dropbox Business accounts can easily scale to accommodate larger teams.

3. **Auditing Your Usage:**
   - Periodically review your team's activity to identify inactive members or unused files.

Setting up a Dropbox team account is the first step toward streamlining collaboration and enhancing productivity. With proper organization, clear permissions, and a focus on security, Dropbox can become a cornerstone of your team's digital toolkit.

3.3.2 Managing Team Members and Roles

Managing team members and roles effectively is a cornerstone of using Dropbox for Teams. This feature allows organizations to ensure seamless collaboration while maintaining control over file access and administrative privileges. In this section, we'll explore how to add and manage team members, assign roles, and use Dropbox's advanced tools to streamline team operations.

Adding Team Members

The first step in managing a Dropbox Team account is inviting members. Administrators can send invitations directly through the admin console. Here's how:

1. **Access the Admin Console**

   Log in to your Dropbox account and navigate to the admin console. From there, go to the **Members** tab.

2. **Send Invitations**

   Click on the **Invite Members** button. You can input email addresses manually or upload a CSV file for bulk invitations. Customize the invitation message to include details about your team's Dropbox usage.

3. **Monitor Invitations**

   Keep track of pending invitations under the **Invitations** section. Resend invitations to ensure all members join promptly.

By proactively managing invitations, administrators can ensure the onboarding process is smooth and efficient.

Assigning Roles to Team Members

Dropbox offers a tiered role system to control member permissions. The three primary roles are:

1. **Team Administrator**
    - Full access to manage all aspects of the account.
    - Capabilities include adding/removing members, adjusting team settings, and viewing activity logs.
    - Ideal for IT managers or senior leaders overseeing organizational Dropbox use.

2. **Support Administrator**
    - Limited administrative privileges, focusing on member management and troubleshooting.
    - Suitable for HR or support staff assisting team members with technical issues.

3. **Team Member**
    - Basic access to shared folders and files within the team.
    - Members cannot change team settings or invite new users.

Assigning the correct roles ensures that sensitive settings and files are only accessible to appropriate personnel.

Managing Permissions within Teams

Once roles are assigned, managing access to specific folders and projects is critical. Dropbox provides several options to fine-tune these permissions:

1. **Shared Folder Permissions**
    - Administrators can assign folder-specific permissions, such as **Editor**, **Viewer**, or **Viewer with Commenting**.

- For confidential projects, restrict access to a small group by setting permissions at the folder level.

2. **Link Sharing Settings**

    - Control whether shared links are open to anyone with the link or restricted to team members.
    - Password-protect sensitive links and set expiration dates for added security.

3. **File Requests**

    - Enable file requests to allow external collaborators to upload files without accessing the entire folder.

With these granular controls, team leaders can ensure that only authorized members have access to sensitive data.

Monitoring Member Activity

Administrators can monitor team activity using Dropbox's **Activity Logs**. These logs provide a detailed view of how members interact with files and folders.

1. **Accessing Logs**

    In the admin console, navigate to the **Activity** section. Filter actions by type, such as file downloads, edits, or shared link creation.

2. **Identifying Anomalies**

    Look for unusual activity, such as multiple downloads in a short period or access from unfamiliar locations. This helps maintain data security.

3. **Exporting Reports**

    Export activity logs for further analysis or compliance purposes. Dropbox allows customization of reports to include specific timeframes or actions.

Adjusting Team Settings

Dropbox's team settings enable administrators to control how members interact with the account. Key options include:

1. **Default Folder Settings**

- Set default permissions for newly created folders. For example, ensure all new folders are private until explicitly shared.

2. **Device Approvals**
    - Limit the number of devices each team member can link to their Dropbox account.
    - Revoke access to old or unauthorized devices from the admin console.

3. **External Sharing Policies**
    - Restrict external sharing of files to protect proprietary information.
    - Enable external sharing for specific team members or folders when collaboration with external partners is essential.

By adjusting these settings, administrators can balance collaboration and security.

Handling Departing Team Members

When a team member leaves, it's crucial to manage their account properly to prevent data loss or unauthorized access. Dropbox provides tools for smooth offboarding:

1. **Account Transfer**
    - Transfer the departing member's files to another team member or administrator. This ensures continuity for ongoing projects.

2. **Revoke Access**
    - Immediately unlink the departing member's devices and remove their access to shared folders.

3. **Audit Activity**
    - Review the member's recent activity to ensure no sensitive data was shared or deleted improperly.

4. **Deactivate Account**
    - Deactivate the account to permanently remove the user from the team.

Efficient offboarding protects organizational data and maintains team integrity.

Fostering Collaboration with Managed Roles

Proper role management enhances collaboration within teams by ensuring clarity and accountability. For example:

- Assign **Editors** to content creators who need full access to shared folders.
- Grant **Viewer** access to stakeholders who only need to review files.
- Use **Support Administrator** roles to delegate technical tasks without compromising sensitive settings.

Tips for Success

- Regularly review team member roles and permissions to adapt to changing responsibilities.
- Host training sessions to educate team members on using Dropbox effectively.
- Use Dropbox's built-in tools, such as **Smart Sync**, to optimize file management.

By leveraging Dropbox's team management features, organizations can foster efficient collaboration while safeguarding their data.

3.3.3 Collaborative Tools for Teams

Dropbox is more than just a file storage and sharing platform—it offers an array of collaborative tools designed to enhance teamwork and streamline workflows. These features are particularly beneficial for organizations looking to improve communication, manage projects effectively, and ensure everyone stays on the same page. In this section, we'll explore the key collaborative tools that Dropbox provides, along with practical examples and best practices for maximizing their impact.

1. Shared Folders for Seamless Collaboration

Shared folders are at the heart of Dropbox's collaborative features. They allow teams to access, edit, and manage files in real time. By setting up shared folders for specific projects or departments, you can eliminate the back-and-forth of email attachments and ensure everyone has the latest version of a file.

- **How to Create a Shared Folder**

- Navigate to your Dropbox dashboard and select "New Folder."
- Name the folder appropriately, such as "Marketing Campaign Q1" or "Client Onboarding Documents."
- Share the folder with team members by entering their email addresses.

- **Best Practices:**
    - Use clear and consistent naming conventions for shared folders to avoid confusion.
    - Set folder permissions based on roles—edit access for contributors and view-only access for stakeholders.

2. Dropbox Paper: Collaborative Document Editing

Dropbox Paper is a powerful tool for teams to create, share, and collaborate on documents in real time. Unlike traditional document editors, Paper integrates seamlessly with other Dropbox features, making it ideal for brainstorming, meeting notes, and project planning.

- **Key Features:**
    - **Real-Time Editing:** Multiple team members can edit a document simultaneously, with changes appearing live.
    - **Task Management:** Add to-do lists and assign tasks directly within the document.
    - **Integration:** Embed files, images, and even YouTube videos directly into a Paper document.
- **Use Case Example:**

    A marketing team can use Dropbox Paper to draft campaign strategies, embed relevant media files, and assign specific tasks to team members—all in one place.

3. Comments and Annotations for Feedback

Dropbox allows users to leave comments and annotations directly on files. This feature eliminates the need for lengthy email threads and helps teams address feedback efficiently.

- **How to Use Comments:**
    - Open a file in Dropbox and select the comment icon.
    - Highlight specific text or areas of an image to leave targeted comments.
    - Tag team members using the "@" symbol to notify them directly.
- **Advantages:**
    - Speeds up the review process by focusing feedback on specific parts of a document.
    - Keeps all communication centralized and easy to track.

4. File Activity and Version History

Dropbox tracks all activity within shared folders and individual files, providing teams with a clear record of who has done what. This transparency is particularly useful for auditing changes and resolving conflicts.

- **Key Features:**
    - **Activity Feed:** Shows when files are uploaded, edited, or shared.
    - **Version History:** Allows users to view and restore previous versions of a file.
- **Best Practices:**
    - Regularly review the activity feed to ensure team members are staying on track.
    - Use version history to recover from accidental changes or deletions.

5. Integrations with Third-Party Apps

Dropbox integrates with numerous third-party tools to enhance team collaboration. These integrations allow teams to work within their preferred software while still leveraging Dropbox's cloud storage capabilities.

- **Popular Integrations:**
    - **Slack:** Share Dropbox files in Slack channels and receive notifications about file activity.
    - **Trello:** Attach Dropbox files to Trello cards for streamlined project management.
    - **Zoom:** Access Dropbox files directly during Zoom meetings for better collaboration.
- **Use Case Example:**

    A product development team can use Trello for task management, Dropbox for file storage, and Slack for communication—all seamlessly integrated.

6. Dropbox Showcase for Presentations

Dropbox Showcase is a tool that allows teams to create visually engaging presentations using files stored in Dropbox. This is especially useful for client-facing teams that need to present polished deliverables.

- **Key Features:**
    - Drag-and-drop functionality to organize files and media into a cohesive presentation.
    - Analytics to track who has viewed the showcase and what they've engaged with.
- **How to Use Showcase:**
    - Create a new showcase and select files from your Dropbox library.
    - Add titles, descriptions, and customizable layouts to enhance the presentation.
    - Share the showcase link with clients or stakeholders.

7. Administrative Controls for Team Management

For team administrators, Dropbox provides tools to manage user permissions, monitor activity, and ensure data security.

- **Key Features:**
    - **User Management:** Add or remove team members and adjust their roles.
    - **Activity Monitoring:** Generate reports on file usage and team activity.
    - **Access Controls:** Set granular permissions for sensitive files or folders.
- **Best Practices:**
    - Conduct regular audits of team activity to ensure compliance with company policies.
    - Use Dropbox's advanced security settings, such as two-factor authentication, to protect sensitive data.

8. Dropbox Spaces: A Digital Workspace

Dropbox Spaces transforms shared folders into collaborative workspaces. Spaces include tools like task management, file previews, and linked content, all in one organized hub.

- **How to Use Dropbox Spaces:**
    - Convert a shared folder into a Space and customize it with descriptions and pinned files.
    - Add tasks and due dates to ensure project milestones are met.
    - Use previews to quickly review files without downloading them.
- **Use Case Example:**

    A project management team can use Dropbox Spaces to organize all resources, track progress, and collaborate in real-time.

9. Benefits of Using Dropbox for Team Collaboration

Dropbox's suite of collaborative tools provides several advantages:

- **Centralized Workflow:** All files, feedback, and tasks are in one place, reducing confusion.

- **Improved Efficiency:** Real-time updates and integrations minimize delays.

- **Enhanced Security:** Robust administrative controls protect sensitive data.

By utilizing these tools effectively, teams can enhance their productivity and ensure successful project outcomes. Whether your organization is a small startup or a large enterprise, Dropbox's collaborative features are designed to meet your needs.

CHAPTER IV
Advanced Features and Integrations

4.1 Version History and File Recovery

4.1.1 Viewing Version History

Dropbox's version history feature is a powerful tool designed to help users track changes, recover earlier iterations, and ensure data integrity across files. Whether you're dealing with accidental edits, unwanted changes, or the need to review previous versions, this feature provides the flexibility to manage your content effectively.

What Is Version History?

Version history allows you to view and restore earlier versions of a file stored in Dropbox. When you modify a file, Dropbox retains copies of previous versions for a specific period, depending on your plan. Basic and Plus accounts maintain version history for 30 days, while Dropbox Professional and Business plans offer extended recovery options, sometimes up to 180 days or more.

This functionality ensures that even if you overwrite a file, accidentally delete critical content, or need to revert to an earlier draft, your previous versions are readily accessible.

Why Is Version History Important?

- **Protection Against Mistakes:** Version history serves as a safety net against accidental changes or deletions. For instance, if you mistakenly overwrite an important file, you can easily recover the original content.

- **Collaboration Management:** In shared folders or team environments, multiple users might work on the same file. Version history enables you to track who made changes and when, fostering accountability and clarity.

- **Restoring Corrupted Files:** If a file becomes corrupted or incompatible due to software issues, version history ensures you can retrieve an uncorrupted version.

- **Efficient File Management:** Reviewing older versions can provide insights into the evolution of a document, which is particularly helpful for projects requiring frequent updates or drafts.

How to View Version History

Dropbox provides a seamless process for accessing version history, whether you're using the web interface, desktop app, or mobile app. Below are step-by-step instructions for each platform:

Accessing Version History on the Web

1. **Log in to Your Dropbox Account:**

   Open a web browser, go to Dropbox.com, and log in with your credentials.

2. **Locate the File:**

   Navigate to the folder where your file is stored. Use the search bar at the top if needed.

3. **Open the File's Options Menu:**

   - Right-click on the file name or hover over it.
   - Select **"Version history"** from the dropdown menu.

CHAPTER IV: ADVANCED FEATURES AND INTEGRATIONS

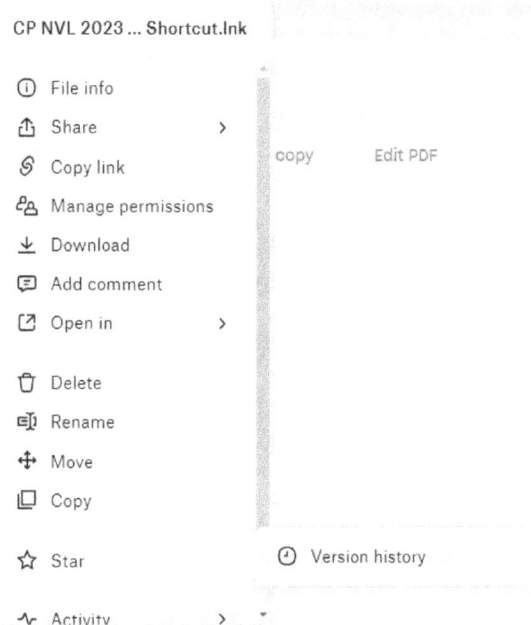

4. **Review Previous Versions:**

    o A new panel will appear, displaying a chronological list of file versions.

    o Each entry includes details such as the date and time of modification, the user who made the changes (for shared files), and the file size.

5. **Preview or Restore a Version:**

    o Click on a version to preview it.

    o To restore, select **"Restore"** next to the desired version. Dropbox will replace the current file with the restored version while retaining the option to revert back if needed.

Viewing Version History in the Desktop App

1. **Open Dropbox on Your Computer:**

    Navigate to your Dropbox folder using File Explorer (Windows) or Finder (Mac).

2. **Right-Click the File:**

- Select the file whose history you wish to view.
- From the context menu, choose **"Version history."**

3. **Explore Versions:**

This action opens your web browser, automatically directing you to the version history page for the selected file. Follow the web instructions to preview or restore the desired version.

Using the Mobile App for Version History

1. **Launch the Dropbox App:**

   Open the Dropbox app on your smartphone or tablet.

2. **Locate the File:**

   Use the search function or navigate through your folders to find the file.

3. **Open the File Menu:**

   - Tap the three-dot menu icon beside the file.
   - Select **"Version history"** from the options.

4. **Review and Restore:**

   - Browse the listed versions and tap on any entry to preview it.
   - To restore, tap the **Restore** button next to the chosen version.

Best Practices for Using Version History

To maximize the benefits of version history, consider the following practices:

- **Regularly Save Changes:** Ensure that all modifications are saved promptly so Dropbox can capture accurate versions.
- **Monitor Shared Files:** For files shared with collaborators, periodically review version history to track edits and prevent accidental overwrites.

- **Archive Key Versions:** When working on critical projects, save and label important milestones by creating a copy in a separate folder. This complements version history and offers additional security.

- **Upgrade for Extended History:** If you frequently need access to older versions or manage large collaborative projects, consider upgrading to a plan with extended version history.

FAQs About Version History

1. **Can I access version history for deleted files?**

   Yes, Dropbox allows you to view and restore versions of deleted files through the Deleted Files section within your account.

2. **Does version history use additional storage?**

   No, previous versions of files do not count against your storage quota.

3. **What happens after the version history period expires?**

   Older versions are automatically deleted once the retention period (e.g., 30 or 180 days) has passed. To preserve specific versions, create a copy before the expiration date.

4. **Is version history available for all file types?**

   Yes, version history applies to all file types stored in Dropbox, including documents, images, and videos.

Conclusion

Dropbox's version history is more than just a convenience; it's a robust feature that enhances file management, supports collaboration, and safeguards against data loss. By understanding how to view and use version history effectively, you can ensure that your work remains organized, secure, and adaptable to changes. Whether you're a casual user or a business professional, mastering this tool is an essential step toward optimizing your Dropbox experience.

4.1.2 Restoring Previous Versions

In the dynamic world of file management, mistakes happen. You may accidentally overwrite a file with incorrect data or find yourself wishing you could revert to an earlier version of a document. Dropbox's **Version History** feature is a lifesaver in these scenarios. It allows users to restore previous versions of files with just a few clicks, ensuring that nothing important is ever permanently lost. This section provides a detailed guide on how to restore earlier file versions, the scenarios where this feature is useful, and best practices for effective version management.

Understanding Version History

Version History in Dropbox stores snapshots of your files whenever they are modified. Depending on your plan, Dropbox retains these versions for a specified period:

- **Basic (Free) Plan**: Versions are kept for up to 30 days.
- **Dropbox Plus, Family, and Professional Plans**: Versions are stored for 30 days, with an optional add-on, Extended Version History, which can retain files for up to a year.
- **Dropbox Business Plans**: Versions are retained for 180 days by default.

Understanding these timeframes is crucial to managing files effectively and ensuring you recover the version you need within the allowed retention period.

Steps to Restore Previous Versions

Restoring previous versions of files is straightforward in Dropbox. Follow these steps:

1. Access the File's Version History

1. Open Dropbox via the web browser or desktop app.
2. Navigate to the file you want to restore.
3. Right-click (or Control-click on Mac) the file and select **Version History** from the dropdown menu.

2. Browse Previous Versions

1. A list of available versions will appear in a timeline or list view.
2. Each version is timestamped with the modification date and the user who made the changes, providing transparency in collaborative environments.
3. Preview the versions to ensure you select the correct one.

3. Restore the Desired Version

1. Once you've identified the desired version, click **Restore**.
2. Dropbox will replace the current version of the file with the selected version while retaining the current version in the Version History.
3. Confirm the restoration, and you're done!

Scenarios Where Restoring Previous Versions Helps

1. Undoing Unintentional Changes

Accidentally deleting key sections of a document or overwriting critical data can be remedied by restoring a previous version.

2. Collaborative Mistakes

In team settings, multiple users may work on a single file. If someone makes unintended changes, Version History helps revert to a version before the error occurred.

3. Ransomware Recovery

Dropbox's versioning can help recover files encrypted by ransomware. By restoring an earlier, unaffected version, you can avoid paying ransom demands.

4. Iterative Workflows

For projects that require constant iteration, such as writing or designing, reverting to earlier drafts can streamline revisions and comparisons.

Mobile Access to Version History

Dropbox also supports file recovery through its mobile app. While the process is slightly different, it is equally user-friendly:

1. Open the Dropbox mobile app and locate your file.
2. Tap the three-dot menu next to the file.
3. Select **Version History** and follow similar steps to restore an earlier version.

Best Practices for Managing Version History

1. Regularly Review Version History

For files with frequent edits, periodically reviewing Version History ensures you can identify changes and recover important data if necessary.

2. Set Clear Collaboration Guidelines

In shared folders, establish ground rules for editing and saving files to minimize accidental overwrites or conflicts.

3. Leverage Extended Version History (if applicable)

If you frequently work on long-term projects, consider upgrading to a plan with extended retention to safeguard your files for longer durations.

4. Integrate with Backup Solutions

While Version History is robust, combining it with a dedicated backup system ensures comprehensive file protection.

Limitations of Version History

While Version History is powerful, it is essential to recognize its limitations:

- **Retention Periods**: Versions are only stored for the specified time based on your plan.
- **File Size Limits**: If a file exceeds Dropbox's maximum size for versioning, it may not be eligible for recovery.
- **Deleted Files**: If a file is permanently deleted, Version History for that file is also erased after 30 days (or the retention limit).

Advanced Features for Restoring Versions

Dropbox offers additional features that enhance the version restoration process:

- **Activity Logs**: For business accounts, administrators can review detailed activity logs to track changes and identify the need for restoration.

- **Third-Party Integration**: Tools like Zapier can automate notifications for file changes, ensuring swift action if restoration is needed.

- **Selective Version Restoration**: Instead of restoring the entire file, you can extract specific content from a version and merge it with the current file manually.

Frequently Asked Questions About Restoring Versions

Q: Can I restore a version from two years ago?

A: Only if you have Extended Version History or an archive that spans that period. Standard plans cap retention at 30 or 180 days. Extended Version History (available with Dropbox Professional or Business plans) can allow access to older versions of files for up to a year.

Q: Does restoring a version affect shared links?

A: No, shared links will automatically reflect the restored version, maintaining seamless collaboration. If someone accesses a shared link after you restore a version, they'll be directed to the newly restored file, ensuring that your collaborators always see the latest content.

Q: Can I recover files deleted by others in shared folders?

A: Yes, as long as the file is within the retention period, and you have the necessary permissions to restore it. Dropbox allows folder owners and collaborators (with appropriate permissions) to recover files that have been deleted, even if the deletion was made by someone else.

Q: What happens to the current version after I restore a previous one?

A: When you restore a previous version, the current version doesn't disappear. Dropbox saves the current version as a separate entry in the version history. This way, you can restore it again if necessary.

Q: Are there any limitations on the number of versions I can access?

A: While there is no strict limit on the number of versions, your access to previous versions depends on your Dropbox plan and the file's version history. The longer you've been editing a file, the more versions you can browse, but the time window for accessing older versions depends on the plan's retention rules.

Q: Can I restore versions for all file types?

A: Most file types are eligible for version history, but there are some exceptions. Large files (over a specific size limit) may not have versioning available. Additionally, some file types (such as those in proprietary formats) may not be as easily versioned as text documents or images. You can check the Dropbox help center for specific file type limitations.

Q: How can I ensure I don't lose important file versions in the future?

A: Regularly back up essential files and consider upgrading to a Dropbox plan with Extended Version History. You can also integrate Dropbox with other cloud storage services or backup tools to have an additional layer of file protection and version control.

Q: What happens if I accidentally restore an old version I didn't want?

A: Don't worry! You can always restore the current version again. Simply go back to the file's Version History and select the most recent version to restore. Dropbox keeps all versions available, so you can cycle through them as needed.

Q: Can I restore previous versions of shared folders?

A: Yes, if you have the necessary permissions, you can restore previous versions of files within shared folders. However, keep in mind that folder permissions and access rights may differ among users, so ensure you have the appropriate access to restore the folder's versions.

Q: How do I know which version of a file is the most recent one?

A: Each version of a file will have a timestamp, which includes the date and time of the last edit. This makes it easy to identify the most recent version and confirm if it is the one you need. For even more detailed tracking, you can review the **Activity** log in Dropbox to see which users made changes and when.

Q: If I delete a file, will I be able to restore its previous versions?

A: Files deleted from your Dropbox can be restored as long as they are within the retention period (30 days for most users or longer for Dropbox Business and Professional plans). Once the file is permanently deleted, its version history is also erased, and it cannot be recovered.

Conclusion

Restoring previous versions is a cornerstone of Dropbox's reliability, offering users peace of mind in managing their digital assets. By mastering this feature, you can recover lost work, undo errors, and maintain seamless workflows. In the next section, we will explore how Dropbox handles **Deleted Files** and techniques for managing them effectively.

4.1.3 Managing Deleted Files

Deleted files in Dropbox are not necessarily gone forever. Dropbox provides a robust file recovery system that allows users to restore accidentally deleted files, manage storage space effectively, and maintain a reliable record of their file management activities. In this section, we'll explore how deleted files are handled in Dropbox, the tools available to restore them, and best practices for managing deleted items efficiently.

Understanding Dropbox's Deleted Files System

When a file or folder is deleted in Dropbox, it's not immediately erased from the cloud. Instead, Dropbox moves the deleted item to a hidden section called **Deleted Files**, where it is stored temporarily. The duration that deleted files remain available depends on the type of Dropbox account you use:

- **Basic and Plus Plans**: Deleted files are retained for up to 30 days.
- **Professional and Business Plans**: These accounts extend the recovery window to 180 days, giving users more flexibility to restore important files.

This system ensures users have ample time to recover files lost due to accidental deletions or unforeseen circumstances, such as system crashes.

Accessing Deleted Files

To manage deleted files, you need to locate them in Dropbox's interface. Here's how to access and view your deleted files:

1. **Via the Web Interface**

    o   Open your Dropbox account in a web browser.

    o   Navigate to the folder where the file was originally stored.

    o   At the top right corner, click the **Show Deleted Files** option. Deleted items will appear with a grayed-out icon, differentiating them from active files.

2. **Via the Mobile App**

    o   Open the Dropbox app on your mobile device.

    o   Go to the folder where the file was located.

    o   Tap the **Options** menu (three dots), and select **View Deleted Files**.

3. **Via the Desktop App**

    o   Open the Dropbox folder on your computer.

    o   Use the **Activity** panel to check for recent deletions, or search for files by name using the search bar.

Restoring Deleted Files

Dropbox makes it simple to recover files directly from the Deleted Files section:

1. Locate the deleted file or folder using the steps above.
2. Click on the deleted item to select it.
3. Choose the **Restore** option from the menu. This action moves the file back to its original location.

Pro Tip: If you're restoring multiple files, you can select them all and restore them in one action, saving time.

Recovering Permanently Deleted Files

Sometimes, files may be permanently deleted from the Deleted Files section after the retention period ends or through a manual deletion. For professional or business accounts, Dropbox offers an **Extended Version History** feature. If this feature is enabled:

- Files deleted beyond the normal retention period can still be recovered.
- Contact Dropbox Support to retrieve these files.

Managing Deleted Files to Optimize Storage

Deleted files still count toward your storage quota until they are permanently removed. To manage this effectively:

1. **Review Your Deleted Files Regularly**
   - Periodically check the Deleted Files section for files that no longer need recovery.
   - Permanently delete files to free up space.
2. **Permanently Deleting Files**
   - Access the Deleted Files section as outlined earlier.
   - Select the items you wish to remove permanently.
   - Click on **Delete Permanently** to ensure they no longer consume storage space.
3. **Use Storage Insights**

- Dropbox's storage insights feature provides a breakdown of your account usage.
- Identify large files that are unnecessarily occupying space and delete them permanently.

Preventing Accidental Deletions

Managing deleted files is easier when preventive measures are in place to avoid accidental deletions. Here are some tips:

1. **Enable File Locking**
   - Dropbox offers a file-locking feature for certain plans, ensuring that critical files cannot be deleted or modified by other collaborators.

2. **Set User Permissions**
   - For shared folders, assign view-only permissions to users who don't need to modify or delete files.

3. **Use File Requests Instead of Direct Uploads**
   - When gathering files from others, use Dropbox's File Request feature. This keeps uploaded content isolated from your main storage, reducing the risk of accidental overwriting or deletion.

Common Issues with Deleted Files and How to Solve Them

1. **File Missing from Deleted Files Section**
   - Check if the file was deleted beyond the retention period. If so, professional or business users can contact support for recovery.
   - Verify that the file wasn't moved to another folder instead of being deleted.

2. **Unable to Restore Files**
   - Ensure there is enough storage space in your Dropbox account to accommodate the restored file.

- Check your internet connection; restoring files requires an active connection to Dropbox servers.

3. **Deleted File Keeps Reappearing**

    - This could happen due to syncing issues between devices. Ensure all devices are synced correctly.
    - Check for third-party app integrations that might be restoring the file automatically.

Best Practices for Managing Deleted Files

1. **Maintain a Clean Deleted Files Section**

    - Regularly clean up this section to prevent unnecessary clutter.
    - Use a folder structure to identify and restore important files more easily.

2. **Enable Notifications for File Deletions**

    - Dropbox can notify you when files are deleted in shared folders, helping you keep track of changes.

3. **Audit Shared Folders**

    - Frequently review shared folder activity to monitor who has been deleting files.
    - Use Dropbox's activity log to track file deletions and restore them promptly if needed.

Conclusion

Managing deleted files in Dropbox is an essential skill for both individual and team users. By leveraging Dropbox's recovery tools and following best practices, you can ensure your important files are safe, restore items with ease, and maintain optimal storage efficiency. Whether you're handling personal files or collaborating on a large project, understanding how to manage deleted files effectively adds an extra layer of confidence to your workflow.

4.2 Offline Access

4.2.1 Setting Up Offline Files

One of the most convenient features of Dropbox is the ability to access files offline. This functionality allows you to keep working or reviewing important documents even without an active internet connection. Whether you're traveling, working in a location with limited connectivity, or simply want the reassurance of having your files readily available, offline access ensures seamless productivity.

In this section, we'll explore step-by-step instructions for setting up offline files on various devices, best practices for efficient use, and troubleshooting common issues.

What Are Offline Files?

Offline files are documents and folders saved locally on your device from Dropbox. While Dropbox primarily operates as a cloud storage service, this feature bridges the gap between cloud accessibility and local reliability. Offline files are synchronized whenever your device reconnects to the internet, ensuring that any changes made offline are automatically updated to the cloud version.

This dual capability—accessing files offline while retaining the benefits of cloud syncing—makes Dropbox a versatile tool for users across industries.

Setting Up Offline Files on Mobile Devices

1. Using Dropbox on iOS

- **Step 1: Open the Dropbox App**

    Launch the Dropbox app on your iPhone or iPad. Ensure you're logged into your account and have access to the files or folders you want to use offline.

- **Step 2: Select Files for Offline Use**

    Navigate to the file or folder you want to save offline. Tap the ellipsis (…) or options menu next to the file name.

- **Step 3: Enable Offline Access**

    Choose the "Make Available Offline" option. A green checkmark will appear next to the file, indicating it's being downloaded for offline use.

- **Step 4: Manage Offline Files**

    Go to the "Offline" tab in the app to view all files currently saved for offline access. This tab provides an overview and allows you to manage offline storage.

2. Using Dropbox on Android

- **Step 1: Launch the App**

    Open the Dropbox app on your Android device and log in.

- **Step 2: Select Files or Folders**

    Browse through your files and folders. Tap and hold on the item you wish to make offline or tap the options menu.

- **Step 3: Choose Offline Availability**

    Select "Make Available Offline." Dropbox will download the file to your device, and an offline icon will appear beside it.

- **Step 4: Verify Storage Usage**

    Visit the app settings to see how much storage space is being used by offline files. This is helpful for ensuring your device doesn't run out of storage.

Setting Up Offline Files on Computers

1. Dropbox Desktop App (Windows/Mac)

The desktop app seamlessly integrates with your operating system, making offline access straightforward:

- **Step 1: Sync Your Account**

    Install and log in to the Dropbox desktop application. By default, the app syncs all files and folders, but you can customize this setting.

- **Step 2: Use Smart Sync**

Dropbox's Smart Sync feature allows you to choose which files are "Local" (stored on your computer) and which are "Online-Only" (stored in the cloud). Right-click on any file or folder in your Dropbox folder, then select "Smart Sync" and "Local" to make it available offline.

- **Step 3: Offline File Management**

    You can still view online-only files in your system file explorer, but they won't take up disk space until downloaded. This ensures you retain control over local storage.

2. **Using Selective Sync**

    - **Step 1: Open Preferences**

        Access the Dropbox preferences/settings panel from your system tray or menu bar.

    - **Step 2: Customize Sync Settings**

        Under the "Sync" tab, choose "Selective Sync." Here, you can select specific folders to sync offline while keeping others cloud-based.

    - **Step 3: Optimize Storage**

        Review your synced folders periodically to remove unnecessary files from local storage.

Best Practices for Using Offline Files

1. **Plan Ahead for Offline Scenarios**

    Before traveling or entering areas with limited connectivity, ensure you've marked critical files as available offline. Verify the downloads are complete by checking the "Offline" tab or viewing the green checkmark beside each file.

2. **Optimize Device Storage**

    Offline files consume local storage, so choose only essential documents to save. Use Dropbox's storage management tools to monitor usage and clear space as needed.

3. **Sync Regularly**

Reconnect to the internet periodically to sync changes made to offline files. This ensures your data remains up-to-date across all devices.

4. **Secure Sensitive Files**

   Offline files can be accessed even without an internet connection, so ensure your device is secured with passwords or biometric locks. Consider encrypting sensitive documents for added protection.

Troubleshooting Offline File Issues

1. Offline Files Not Downloading

- Check your internet connection and retry the download process.
- Ensure you have sufficient storage space on your device.
- Update the Dropbox app to the latest version.

2. Changes Not Syncing After Reconnection

- Confirm that Dropbox is running and connected to the internet.
- Check for conflicts between offline edits and cloud versions. Dropbox will alert you of any discrepancies, allowing you to resolve them manually.

3. Files Missing from Offline Tab

- Verify that the files were marked for offline access.
- Check the app settings to ensure offline storage hasn't been disabled.

Benefits of Offline Files

Using offline files ensures that you're always prepared, even in the most unpredictable circumstances. Whether you're a student working on assignments, a professional reviewing documents on the go, or an entrepreneur presenting to clients in remote locations, offline access ensures uninterrupted productivity.

By following these steps and best practices, you'll master Dropbox's offline file functionality, unlocking a critical feature for seamless, reliable access to your most important data.

4.2.2 Managing Offline Preferences

Dropbox's offline feature is a game-changer for accessing your files when you're not connected to the internet. Properly managing offline preferences ensures that you have everything you need while staying efficient with storage space. This section explores how to configure offline settings effectively, prioritize important files, and manage the synchronization process seamlessly.

Understanding Offline Preferences

Dropbox offers the ability to mark specific files and folders for offline use, allowing you to access them even without an active internet connection. This feature is available across mobile apps and desktop versions, each with unique settings and considerations. Offline preferences can be tailored to match your needs, whether for work, school, or personal projects.

Key benefits include:

- **Accessibility:** Immediate access to critical files without relying on connectivity.
- **Efficiency:** Reduced data usage when working in limited-bandwidth situations.
- **Convenience:** Avoid disruptions during travel or in areas with poor signal.

Steps to Manage Offline Preferences on Desktop

1. Selecting Files for Offline Access

Dropbox on desktop allows you to designate files or folders for offline use via the Dropbox folder or application interface.

- **Step 1:** Open the Dropbox desktop app or navigate to your Dropbox folder.
- **Step 2:** Right-click the desired file or folder.
- **Step 3:** Select **Make Available Offline** (this may also appear as "Smart Sync" depending on your plan).

This action ensures that a local copy of the file is stored on your hard drive for offline access.

2. Customizing Smart Sync Settings

Smart Sync is an advanced feature in Dropbox that helps manage storage by keeping non-essential files online-only while syncing critical ones locally.

- **Automatic Settings:** Allow Dropbox to determine which files to store locally based on frequency of use.
- **Manual Settings:** You can override automatic suggestions by setting files to **Local** (offline) or **Online Only** manually.

This functionality strikes a balance between maintaining local storage space and having essential files at your fingertips.

3. Checking Sync Status

Ensure that your files are fully downloaded and ready for offline use.

- Look for a **green checkmark icon** indicating successful sync.
- If files display a **gray cloud icon**, they are online-only and won't be accessible offline.

Managing Offline Preferences on Mobile

1. Marking Files for Offline Use

The Dropbox mobile app simplifies offline management with intuitive controls.

- **Step 1:** Open the Dropbox app and navigate to the desired file or folder.
- **Step 2:** Tap the three-dot menu icon next to the file name.
- **Step 3:** Select **Make Available Offline** to save it to your device.

These files will be stored within the app's local storage, allowing for seamless access without consuming excessive device space.

2. Prioritizing Space-Efficient Downloads

To avoid overloading your mobile device's storage, prioritize downloading smaller or frequently-used files. You can also clear offline files when no longer needed by returning to the three-dot menu and selecting **Remove from Device**.

3. Managing Offline Preferences in Settings

Dropbox's app settings provide greater control over offline options.

- Go to **Settings > Offline Files.**
- View all files marked for offline access in one place.
- Adjust download preferences, such as enabling downloads only over Wi-Fi to save mobile data.

Best Practices for Offline Access Management

1. Keep Critical Files Up-to-Date

Always verify that your offline files are the latest versions, especially for collaborative projects. Dropbox automatically updates offline files when connected to the internet, but you can force a sync by refreshing manually.

2. Monitor Storage Usage

Offline files consume device storage, so regularly review and delete unnecessary files. Use Dropbox's built-in storage tracker to manage space effectively.

3. Set Priorities for Work and Travel

Before a long trip or remote work session, pre-download all essential files. Double-check their offline status to prevent last-minute surprises.

4. Plan for Offline Collaboration

If you're working on a shared file, ensure that collaborators are aware of offline edits. Dropbox syncs changes once the device reconnects, but timing conflicts can lead to duplicate versions. Use Dropbox Paper or comments to minimize confusion.

Troubleshooting Offline Access

1. File Not Accessible Offline

If a file marked for offline use isn't available:

- Check for pending sync icons (e.g., rotating arrows).
- Ensure you're logged into the correct Dropbox account.
- Verify that the file wasn't removed or relocated.

2. Sync Errors

Errors during synchronization are often caused by:

- Insufficient storage space on your device.
- Weak or unstable internet connections during sync setup.
- Corrupted files that need re-uploading or re-downloading.

3. Reverting to Default Settings

If offline preferences seem overly complex, reset to default settings:

- Disable offline access for all files.
- Re-enable only essential files and folders.

Enhancing Your Offline Experience

Dropbox continues to improve its offline capabilities, with features like:

- **Offline Collaboration Updates:** Allowing team members to tag each other or leave comments offline, syncing automatically once online.
- **Automatic Priority Downloads:** Identifying and prioritizing the files most relevant to your recent activity.

As Dropbox evolves, staying updated on new offline tools will enhance your productivity and ensure uninterrupted access to your content.

By mastering offline preferences, you can leverage Dropbox's power to its fullest, ensuring that your files are accessible, secure, and organized no matter where you are.

4.2.3 Troubleshooting Offline Sync Issues

Dropbox's offline access feature allows users to work on their files without an internet connection, ensuring productivity even in areas with limited connectivity. However, like any technology, offline sync may encounter issues that can disrupt workflow. This section provides a comprehensive guide to identifying and resolving offline sync issues, ensuring a seamless Dropbox experience.

Understanding Common Offline Sync Problems

Before diving into solutions, it's crucial to understand the common issues that may arise:

1. **Files Not Syncing Offline**

   Files marked for offline access may not appear available when there is no internet connection.

2. **Outdated Versions**

   Edits made offline may not sync correctly once the internet connection is restored, leading to version conflicts.

3. **Storage Limitations**

   Insufficient storage on your device may prevent files from downloading for offline use.

4. **Corrupted Downloads**

   Files may fail to open if they were corrupted during the download process.

5. **App Crashes**

   The Dropbox app may crash or freeze while accessing offline files, disrupting your workflow.

Step-by-Step Troubleshooting

Step 1: Verify Offline File Settings

- **Ensure Offline Access is Enabled:**

  Go to the Dropbox app on your device, locate the file or folder in question, and verify that it is marked for offline access. You should see a green icon indicating the file is ready offline.

- **Re-enable Offline Access:**

  If the offline setting is active but the file isn't accessible, disable and re-enable offline access.

Step 2: Check Device Storage

- **Assess Available Space:**

  Low storage can prevent files from being downloaded for offline use. Check your device's storage settings and clear unnecessary files to free up space.

- **Adjust Dropbox Sync Settings:**

  In the Dropbox app settings, ensure the app has permission to use sufficient storage on your device.

Step 3: Resolve Network Transition Issues

- **Reconnecting to the Internet:**

  If sync doesn't occur after reconnecting to the internet, manually refresh the Dropbox app or restart your device.

- **Update Pending Files:**

  Sometimes, edits made offline are placed in a queue. Open the Dropbox app and ensure that pending uploads are processed.

Step 4: Address App Performance Problems

- **Update the Dropbox App:**

  Ensure you are using the latest version of the app. Older versions may contain bugs that affect offline functionality.

- **Clear the App Cache:**

  Excessive cache files may disrupt app performance. Clear the cache in the app settings.

- **Reinstall Dropbox:**

    If the app continues to crash or freeze, uninstall and reinstall it. Make sure to reconfigure offline access for your files.

Step 5: Handle File Corruption

- **Re-download Corrupted Files:**

    If a file fails to open, remove it from offline access and re-download it.

- **Check File Format Compatibility:**

    Ensure that the file format is supported by both Dropbox and your device's apps.

Preventing Offline Sync Issues

Maintain Regular App Updates

Dropbox frequently updates its app to address bugs and improve performance. Enable automatic updates to ensure you always have the latest features and fixes.

Monitor Device Storage

Regularly monitor your device's storage capacity to prevent sync interruptions. Consider using an external storage device or cloud backup for additional space.

Enable Background Syncing

Allow Dropbox to sync in the background by adjusting your device's battery optimization settings. This ensures files are downloaded and updated even when the app isn't actively open.

Keep Offline Files Organized

Avoid clutter by periodically reviewing and managing offline files. Remove files you no longer need offline to free up storage and reduce app workload.

Advanced Solutions for Persistent Issues

If the basic troubleshooting steps don't resolve the issue, consider these advanced options:

Check Permissions

Ensure Dropbox has the necessary permissions on your device to access storage and operate offline.

Review System Updates

Sometimes, system updates can disrupt app functionality. Check for recent updates to your device's operating system and ensure compatibility with the Dropbox app.

Use the Web Version as a Backup

If offline access isn't working on your mobile or desktop app, the web version of Dropbox can serve as a temporary solution once you regain internet access.

Contact Dropbox Support

For unresolved issues, reach out to Dropbox's support team. Provide detailed information about the problem, including device type, app version, and any error messages encountered.

Case Study: Resolving a Real-World Issue

Scenario:
A user traveling in a remote area downloaded several project files for offline access. Upon attempting to open the files, they found some were missing while others wouldn't load.

Resolution Steps:

1. Checked device storage and freed up additional space by deleting unused apps.
2. Re-enabled offline access for the missing files.
3. Updated the Dropbox app and cleared its cache.
4. Ensured the device had the latest operating system updates.
5. Successfully re-downloaded files, resolving the issue.

This example highlights the importance of proactive maintenance and following systematic troubleshooting steps.

Conclusion

Offline access is a powerful feature that enhances Dropbox's usability in low-connectivity scenarios. By understanding potential issues and implementing these troubleshooting strategies, users can ensure their files are always accessible and their productivity remains uninterrupted. Whether you're working on critical projects or simply accessing personal documents, these tips will help you make the most of Dropbox's offline capabilities.

4.3 Integrating Dropbox with Other Tools

4.3.1 Integrations with Google Workspace

Integrating Dropbox with Google Workspace brings the power of cloud storage and productivity tools together, creating a seamless experience for users to manage, collaborate, and share files. This integration is particularly beneficial for teams and individuals who regularly use Google Docs, Sheets, Slides, and Gmail alongside Dropbox. Below, we'll explore how to connect Dropbox to Google Workspace, key benefits of this integration, and practical tips for optimizing its use.

Connecting Dropbox to Google Workspace

To take full advantage of this integration, you need to connect Dropbox to your Google Workspace account. Here's how to get started:

1. **Enable the Integration in Dropbox**:
    - Log in to your Dropbox account on the web.
    - Navigate to **Settings** > **Connected Apps**.
    - Look for "Google Workspace" in the list of available integrations and click **Connect**.

2. **Authorize the Connection**:
    - You'll be redirected to Google's authentication page.
    - Select the Google account you want to link with Dropbox.
    - Grant the necessary permissions to allow Dropbox access to your Google Workspace files and tools.

3. **Start Using the Integration**:
    - Once the connection is established, you can start creating, editing, and saving Google Docs, Sheets, and Slides directly within your Dropbox folders.

Key Benefits of Integrating Dropbox with Google Workspace

This integration offers several advantages that streamline workflows and enhance productivity:

1. **Centralized File Management**:

    o   With Dropbox, you can store, organize, and manage all your Google Workspace files in one place.

    o   This eliminates the need to switch between multiple platforms, saving time and effort.

2. **Collaborative Editing**:

    o   Open and edit Google Docs, Sheets, and Slides directly from Dropbox.

    o   Changes made in Dropbox are automatically saved in real-time to your Google account, ensuring seamless collaboration.

3. **Easy Sharing and Permissions**:

    o   Share Google Workspace files stored in Dropbox with just a few clicks.

    o   Dropbox's sharing features allow you to control access levels, set expiration dates for links, and track file activity.

4. **Enhanced Workflow Efficiency**:

    o   Access Google Workspace files alongside other project materials stored in Dropbox, keeping everything in context.

    o   Use Dropbox's tagging and search features to quickly find the files you need, even if they are Google Workspace documents.

5. **Secure Storage and Backup**:

    o   Files stored in Dropbox benefit from its robust security measures, including encryption, two-factor authentication, and backup options.

    o   This adds an extra layer of protection to your Google Workspace documents.

How to Use the Integration Effectively

To maximize the potential of Dropbox and Google Workspace, consider the following best practices:

1. **Organize Files into Logical Folders**:
    - Create specific folders in Dropbox for different projects or departments.
    - Save Google Docs, Sheets, and Slides in these folders to maintain a clear organizational structure.

2. **Leverage Shared Folders for Team Collaboration**:
    - Use Dropbox's shared folders to collaborate on Google Workspace files with your team.
    - Assign appropriate permissions to ensure that team members can view or edit files as needed.

3. **Use Google Workspace for Real-Time Collaboration**:
    - For documents requiring simultaneous editing, open Google Docs, Sheets, or Slides from Dropbox to enable real-time collaboration.
    - Changes are updated instantly, allowing for smoother teamwork.

4. **Enable Offline Access for Google Workspace Files**:
    - Set up offline access for Dropbox and Google Workspace to work on files even without an internet connection.
    - Changes will sync automatically once you reconnect to the internet.

5. **Search Smartly**:
    - Utilize Dropbox's advanced search feature to find Google Workspace files by name, content, or file type.
    - Tag files with relevant keywords to make searching faster.

6. **Integrate Gmail with Dropbox**:
    - Attach Dropbox files directly from Gmail, saving time and effort.

- Save email attachments to Dropbox with a single click for easy file management.

Common Use Cases for the Integration

1. **Project Management**:
   - Store project-related Google Docs, Sheets, and Slides in Dropbox alongside other assets like images, PDFs, and videos.
   - Use shared folders to keep the entire team updated on project progress.

2. **Content Creation**:
   - Draft blog posts or articles using Google Docs stored in Dropbox.
   - Collaborate with editors and designers by sharing a single Dropbox folder containing drafts, graphics, and feedback.

3. **Budgeting and Financial Analysis**:
   - Create and update budgets in Google Sheets while storing them securely in Dropbox.
   - Share these Sheets with stakeholders and use Dropbox's file activity tracking to monitor who has viewed or edited them.

4. **Presentations and Proposals**:
   - Design presentations using Google Slides and organize them in Dropbox for easy access during meetings.
   - Use Dropbox's offline mode to present even in areas with poor internet connectivity.

Troubleshooting Integration Issues

If you encounter problems while using the Dropbox and Google Workspace integration, here are some solutions:

1. **Reauthorize the Connection**:

- If you're unable to access Google Workspace files from Dropbox, try reauthorizing the connection through your Dropbox settings.

2. **Check File Permissions**:
   - Ensure that the files you're trying to edit or share have the correct permissions in both Google Workspace and Dropbox.

3. **Update Apps**:
   - Keep both Dropbox and Google Workspace apps up to date to avoid compatibility issues.

4. **Contact Support**:
   - For persistent problems, reach out to Dropbox or Google Workspace support for assistance.

Integrating Dropbox with Google Workspace is a powerful way to enhance productivity and streamline workflows. Whether you're an individual user or part of a team, this integration allows you to work smarter by combining the best features of both platforms. Take advantage of the tips and techniques outlined above to get the most out of this seamless collaboration.

4.3.2 Using Dropbox with Microsoft Office

Integrating Dropbox with Microsoft Office allows users to seamlessly store, share, and collaborate on documents, spreadsheets, and presentations. This integration optimizes workflows for individuals and teams, especially those who frequently use Office tools like Word, Excel, and PowerPoint. In this section, we will explore how to connect Dropbox to Microsoft Office, work on files directly from Dropbox, and utilize advanced collaboration features.

Connecting Dropbox to Microsoft Office

The first step to using Dropbox with Microsoft Office is establishing the integration. Dropbox and Office have built-in compatibility, making the process straightforward. Here's how to get started:

1. **Ensure Compatibility**:
   - Verify that your Office version supports cloud integration (Office 365 or Microsoft 2019/2021 is recommended).
   - Ensure you have an active Dropbox account and have installed the Dropbox app on your desktop or mobile device.

2. **Link Your Accounts**:
   - **Desktop**:
     - Open the Dropbox desktop app and sign in.
     - Navigate to the settings menu and find the "Connected Apps" section.
     - Select "Microsoft Office" and follow the on-screen instructions to link your Office account.
   - **Mobile**:
     - Open the Dropbox mobile app.
     - Tap on the menu (usually three horizontal lines) and select "Settings."
     - Find the "Link with Microsoft Office" option and authorize the connection.

3. **Test the Integration**:
   - Open any Microsoft Office file stored in Dropbox. You should see an option to edit it directly in the corresponding Office app (e.g., Word for .docx files).

Working with Office Files in Dropbox

Once the integration is set up, you can work on Office files directly from Dropbox, whether on a desktop, mobile, or web platform.

1. Editing Documents in Real Time

Dropbox allows real-time editing of Word, Excel, and PowerPoint files.

- **Desktop**: Double-click a file in your Dropbox folder. It will open in the corresponding Office application. Any changes you make are saved directly to Dropbox.

- **Web**: Open the Dropbox website, locate your file, and select "Open with Microsoft Office Online." This option is ideal for quick edits without downloading files.

- **Mobile**: Use the Dropbox mobile app to open a file, which will automatically redirect you to the Office app installed on your device.

2. Auto-Saving and Syncing

- Any edits made to Office files are automatically saved in Dropbox. This eliminates the risk of losing work due to software crashes or power outages.

- Dropbox syncs changes across all linked devices, ensuring you always access the latest version of your file.

3. Co-Authoring Documents

Dropbox and Microsoft Office support co-authoring, enabling multiple users to work on the same document simultaneously.

- Share the file with collaborators via Dropbox.

- Open the file in Office Online or a desktop app. All edits are synchronized in real-time, and you can see who is editing each section.

- Use comments and track changes to enhance communication during collaborative projects.

Organizing and Sharing Office Files in Dropbox

Dropbox offers advanced file organization and sharing options, especially useful for managing Office documents.

1. Folder Organization

- Create dedicated folders for different types of Office files, such as "Reports" for Word documents or "Budget Sheets" for Excel files.

- Use color-coded folder tags to visually distinguish between work and personal files.

2. File Requests

- If you need Office files from others, use Dropbox's "File Request" feature. This tool lets users upload files directly to your Dropbox account, even if they don't have an account themselves.

3. Sharing Permissions

- Share files or folders with specific individuals by sending an invite link.

- Set permissions such as "View Only" or "Can Edit" to control access levels.

- Password-protect links or set expiration dates for additional security.

Advanced Collaboration Tools

Dropbox's integration with Microsoft Office isn't just about editing and saving files. It also enhances collaboration through advanced tools.

1. Commenting and Feedback

- Add comments to specific sections of a Word document or PowerPoint slide.

- Tag collaborators directly by using "@" followed by their name. Tagged individuals will receive notifications for quick feedback.

2. Task Assignments

- Assign tasks within Office files using Dropbox's task management feature. For example, in a shared Excel sheet, you can assign a specific cell or section to a teammate.

3. Version Control

- Use Dropbox's version history to view or revert to previous iterations of an Office document. This is particularly useful for tracking edits in collaborative projects.

- Combine this with Office's "Track Changes" feature for detailed revision tracking.

Integrating Dropbox with Office 365 Online

For users of Office 365, Dropbox offers seamless integration for cloud-based workflows.

1. Accessing Files in Office 365

- Log in to your Office 365 account.
- Use the "Open from Dropbox" option when selecting files to work on directly within Office Online.

2. Saving Back to Dropbox

- After editing files in Office 365, save them directly to your Dropbox without needing to download and re-upload them.

3. Using Add-Ins

- Install the Dropbox add-in for Office 365. This allows you to attach Dropbox files to emails or insert them directly into Word, Excel, or PowerPoint documents without leaving the app.

Tips for Optimizing the Integration

- **Enable Offline Mode**: For Office files, enable offline access in Dropbox so you can work without an internet connection. Changes will sync once you're back online.
- **Regularly Review Shared Links**: Ensure that files shared via Dropbox links still have appropriate permissions and update them as needed.
- **Use Naming Conventions**: Adopt a consistent naming system for Office files to avoid confusion, especially in collaborative projects.

By leveraging the full potential of Dropbox's integration with Microsoft Office, users can streamline their workflows, enhance collaboration, and increase productivity. This powerful combination ensures that you can manage and share your Office documents with confidence and ease.

4.3.3 Connecting Dropbox to Slack and Trello

In today's digital workplace, collaboration and task management tools are crucial for seamless communication and productivity. Dropbox integrates seamlessly with platforms like Slack and Trello, offering enhanced capabilities for file sharing, task organization, and team collaboration. This section will guide you through connecting Dropbox with these tools and maximizing their potential for your workflow.

Why Integrate Dropbox with Slack and Trello?

Dropbox's integrations with Slack and Trello simplify workflows by enabling:

- **Effortless File Sharing:** Share Dropbox files directly in Slack conversations or Trello cards without leaving the platform.
- **Improved Collaboration:** Collaborate on files in real-time while keeping discussions and tasks organized.
- **Centralized Workflow Management:** Link Dropbox files to tasks and projects, ensuring everyone on the team has access to the right resources.
- **Time Savings:** Reduce the need to switch between apps and minimize repetitive actions.

Let's dive into how you can set up these integrations and use them effectively.

Connecting Dropbox to Slack

Slack is a powerful communication tool that keeps teams connected through channels and direct messages. Dropbox's integration with Slack allows you to share, search, and preview files with ease.

Step 1: Linking Dropbox to Slack

1. Open your Dropbox account in a web browser and navigate to the **App Center**.
2. Search for **Slack** in the integrations directory.

3. Click on the Slack app and select **Connect to Slack**.
4. Log in to your Slack workspace and authorize Dropbox.
5. Choose the Slack channels or direct messages you want Dropbox to access.

Once the integration is enabled, you can start sharing files directly from Dropbox in your Slack workspace.

Step 2: Sharing Files in Slack

To share a Dropbox file in Slack:

- Type /dropbox in any Slack channel or direct message, followed by the file name. Dropbox will search your files and provide a shareable link.
- Alternatively, go to the file in Dropbox, click **Share**, and select **Send to Slack**.

Step 3: Previewing Files in Slack

Dropbox files shared in Slack automatically generate previews, allowing team members to review content without downloading the file. Supported file types include PDFs, images, and Microsoft Office documents.

Step 4: Managing File Permissions

When sharing a Dropbox file in Slack, you can adjust permissions to control who can view or edit the file. Simply click **Manage Access** in Dropbox before sharing the link.

Connecting Dropbox to Trello

Trello is a popular project management tool that uses boards, lists, and cards to organize tasks. Integrating Dropbox with Trello streamlines project workflows by attaching relevant files to specific tasks.

Step 1: Linking Dropbox to Trello

1. Open your Trello board and navigate to the **Power-Ups** section in the board menu.
2. Search for **Dropbox** in the Power-Up directory and click **Add Power-Up**.
3. Authorize Dropbox to connect with Trello by logging into your account.

Once connected, Dropbox will be available as an attachment option for Trello cards.

Step 2: Attaching Files to Trello Cards

To attach a Dropbox file to a Trello card:

- Open a card on your Trello board.
- Click on **Attachments** and select **Dropbox**.
- Browse your Dropbox folders to select the file you want to attach.

The file will appear as a clickable link on the Trello card, ensuring that team members can access it instantly.

Step 3: Using Dropbox Links in Trello

If you prefer to share a file via a link:

- Copy the Dropbox shareable link and paste it into the card's description or comments section.
- Trello will automatically generate a preview of the file if supported.

Step 4: Organizing and Updating Files

Files attached from Dropbox remain up-to-date. Any changes made in Dropbox are reflected in the linked Trello card, reducing the risk of outdated information.

Best Practices for Using Dropbox with Slack and Trello

To maximize the benefits of these integrations, consider the following tips:

1. Establish Naming Conventions

Clear and consistent file names in Dropbox make it easier to locate and share files in Slack and Trello. Use names that reflect the file's purpose and project.

2. Use Shared Folders for Team Projects

Create Dropbox shared folders for project files and link these folders in relevant Trello boards or Slack channels. This ensures everyone has access to the same resources.

3. Set Permissions Thoughtfully

Before sharing files, review access permissions to ensure the right people can view or edit them. Avoid granting unnecessary permissions to maintain data security.

4. Leverage Previews and Comments

Encourage team members to use file previews and comments in Slack and Trello for quick feedback. This reduces the need for long email threads or separate review tools.

5. Keep Tools Updated

Ensure that both Dropbox and the connected apps are updated to the latest versions. This prevents compatibility issues and unlocks new features.

Troubleshooting Dropbox Integrations

While Dropbox integrations with Slack and Trello are designed to be user-friendly, occasional issues may arise. Here's how to handle common problems:

Issue 1: Integration Not Working

- Verify that Dropbox, Slack, or Trello accounts are properly linked.
- Check your internet connection and try reconnecting the apps.

Issue 2: File Previews Not Displaying

- Ensure the file type is supported for previews in Slack or Trello.
- Re-upload the file to Dropbox if it appears corrupted.

Issue 3: Permissions Errors

- Confirm that the file permissions in Dropbox match your sharing intentions.
- Update the sharing link or card attachment if access needs to be adjusted.

Conclusion

Integrating Dropbox with Slack and Trello elevates your productivity by bringing file management, communication, and task organization into one seamless workflow. By following the steps outlined in this section and adopting the best practices shared, you can simplify collaboration and stay focused on achieving your goals. Whether you're sharing a proposal in Slack or attaching a presentation to a Trello card, Dropbox ensures your files are always accessible, secure, and up-to-date.

CHAPTER V
Security and Privacy

5.1 Securing Your Account

5.1.1 Enabling Two-Factor Authentication

Securing your Dropbox account is crucial in today's digital age, where cyber threats and hacking attempts are more prevalent than ever. One of the most effective ways to protect your account is by enabling **Two-Factor Authentication (2FA)**. This security feature adds an additional layer of defense, ensuring that even if someone gains access to your password, they cannot log in without the second authentication factor.

What is Two-Factor Authentication?

Two-Factor Authentication, commonly abbreviated as 2FA, is a security measure that requires two separate methods of verifying your identity before granting access to your account. The first factor is something you know, such as your password. The second factor is something you have, such as a code sent to your mobile device. This combination significantly reduces the risk of unauthorized access.

Benefits of Two-Factor Authentication on Dropbox

Dropbox provides 2FA to enhance your account's security. Here are the key advantages:

1. **Increased Security:** Even if your password is compromised, attackers cannot access your account without the second factor.
2. **Protection Against Phishing:** If you accidentally provide your password to a fake login page, 2FA prevents further access.

3. **Ease of Use:** Dropbox's 2FA setup process is straightforward, making it accessible for users of all technical backgrounds.

4. **Customizable Options:** Dropbox allows you to choose between various authentication methods, providing flexibility for your needs.

How to Enable Two-Factor Authentication

Follow these steps to set up 2FA on your Dropbox account:

1. **Sign In to Your Dropbox Account:**

    Log in to your Dropbox account on the web. Navigate to the **Account Settings** page.

2. **Access the Security Tab:**

    Click on the **Security** tab in your account settings. Here, you will find an option labeled **Two-Factor Authentication**.

3. **Start the Setup Process:**

    Click **Enable Two-Factor Authentication**. Dropbox will prompt you to confirm your password for security purposes.

4. **Choose Your Authentication Method:**

    Dropbox offers two primary methods for receiving the second factor:

    - **Text Messages (SMS):** A code is sent to your phone via SMS.
    - **Authentication Apps:** Apps like Google Authenticator or Authy generate time-sensitive codes.

Select the method that works best for you. Authentication apps are generally more secure as they don't rely on your phone number, which can be vulnerable to SIM-swapping attacks.

5. **Verify Your Device:**

    - For SMS, enter the code sent to your phone to confirm.
    - For an authentication app, scan the QR code provided by Dropbox, and enter the code generated by the app.

6. **Save Backup Codes:**

   Dropbox will provide a set of **backup codes**. These codes are essential if you lose access to your phone or app. Save them in a secure location, such as a password manager.

Best Practices for Using Two-Factor Authentication

While enabling 2FA adds significant security, following these best practices ensures optimal protection:

1. **Use an Authentication App Instead of SMS:**

   Authentication apps are more secure than SMS because they are not susceptible to SIM-swapping attacks, where attackers manipulate telecom providers to gain access to your phone number.

2. **Keep Backup Codes Safe:**

   Store your backup codes in a secure, offline location. Avoid saving them on your device, as they could be accessed if your device is compromised.

3. **Enable Notifications for Suspicious Activity:**

   Dropbox provides alerts for unusual account activities. Enable these notifications to stay informed of any unauthorized access attempts.

4. **Regularly Update Your Phone Number:**

   If you change your phone number, update it in your Dropbox settings immediately to avoid losing access to your 2FA codes.

Troubleshooting Common Issues with 2FA

While setting up or using 2FA, you may encounter some common problems. Here's how to address them:

1. **I Lost My Authentication Device:**

   Use your backup codes to regain access. If you've lost these too, contact Dropbox support for assistance.

2. **The Code Isn't Working:**

    o   Ensure the time on your device matches the time on Dropbox's servers.

    o   For authentication apps, make sure you are using the most recent code, as they refresh every 30 seconds.

3. **I Changed My Phone Number:**

    If you've already updated your number in Dropbox, you'll receive codes on your new phone. Otherwise, use your backup codes to log in and update your phone number.

Why You Should Enable 2FA Now

Procrastinating on enabling 2FA leaves your account vulnerable to cyber threats. Here's why you should set it up today:

1. **Prevent Account Hijacking:** The internet is rife with phishing attempts, keylogging software, and brute-force attacks. 2FA acts as a shield against all these threats.

2. **Peace of Mind:** Knowing that your sensitive files and personal data are secure provides immense relief.

3. **Industry Standard:** Many leading platforms, including Dropbox, recommend or even require 2FA for account security.

Conclusion

Two-Factor Authentication is an essential tool in securing your Dropbox account. It's easy to set up, highly effective, and provides an extra layer of protection that ensures your files remain private and secure. By enabling 2FA today, you take a proactive step toward safeguarding your digital assets in an increasingly connected world.

5.1.2 Setting Strong Passwords

A strong password is the cornerstone of account security, particularly for cloud storage services like Dropbox that safeguard sensitive personal and professional data. Weak passwords are one of the most common vulnerabilities exploited by attackers. This section will guide you on how to create strong passwords, why they matter, and strategies to maintain secure password practices.

The Importance of Strong Passwords

Passwords act as the first line of defense against unauthorized access to your Dropbox account. A weak password can be cracked in seconds by sophisticated hacking techniques, putting your sensitive files, financial documents, or business-critical data at risk. Strong passwords significantly reduce the likelihood of a successful attack by increasing the complexity and time required for malicious actors to breach your account.

Key Characteristics of a Strong Password

To ensure the security of your Dropbox account, your password should adhere to these principles:

1. **Length**: Longer passwords are exponentially more secure than shorter ones. Aim for a minimum of 12-16 characters.

2. **Complexity**: Include a mix of:
    - Uppercase letters (e.g., A, B, C)
    - Lowercase letters (e.g., a, b, c)
    - Numbers (e.g., 1, 2, 3)
    - Special characters (e.g., @, #, $, %)

3. **Unpredictability**: Avoid using predictable information like your name, birthday, or commonly used words. For instance, passwords like "Password123" or "Dropbox2024" are weak and vulnerable.

4. **Uniqueness**: Do not reuse passwords across multiple platforms. A breach on one service could compromise all accounts sharing the same password.

How to Create Strong Passwords

1. Use a Password Manager

Password managers are excellent tools for generating and storing strong passwords. They create random combinations of letters, numbers, and symbols, ensuring unpredictability. Additionally, they save these passwords securely, so you only need to remember a single master password. Popular password managers include LastPass, Dashlane, and 1Password.

2. Mnemonic Techniques

If you prefer to remember your passwords manually, use a memorable phrase and incorporate complexity. For example:

- Take the phrase "I love Dropbox for cloud storage" and convert it into a password like **"IL0v3Dr0pb@x4Cl0ud!"**.

3. Randomized Password Generators

Online tools like those provided by Dropbox or security websites can create strong, randomized passwords instantly. Avoid saving these passwords in unsecured locations.

4. Avoid Patterns and Repetition

Passwords like "abcd1234" or "qwerty" are easily guessable due to their patterns. Similarly, avoid repeating characters like "aaaa" or "123123".

Common Mistakes to Avoid

1. **Reusing Old Passwords**: Avoid using passwords you've used before, even if it was years ago.
2. **Sharing Your Password**: Never share your password with others, even trusted individuals. Use secure file-sharing features within Dropbox instead.
3. **Writing Passwords Down**: Storing passwords in easily accessible locations, such as a sticky note or a plain text file on your computer, undermines their security.
4. **Using Default or Pre-Set Passwords**: Change any default password immediately upon setting up a new account.

Testing Password Strength

Many platforms, including Dropbox, provide a password strength checker during account setup or password updates. You can also use third-party tools like "How Secure Is My Password?" to evaluate your password's resilience against attacks. A strong password should require billions of years to crack using modern computational power.

Best Practices for Maintaining Secure Passwords

1. Regular Updates

Change your Dropbox password every 6-12 months, especially if you suspect it may have been compromised. Regular updates reduce the risk of long-term breaches.

2. Monitor for Breaches

Use services like Have I Been Pwned to check if your email address or password has been exposed in any data breaches. If so, immediately update your Dropbox password.

3. Use Two-Factor Authentication (2FA)

As discussed in section 5.1.1, enabling 2FA adds an additional security layer, ensuring that even if your password is compromised, unauthorized access remains unlikely.

4. Avoid Auto-Saving Passwords on Shared Devices

While browsers offer the convenience of saving passwords, avoid doing so on devices that are shared or unsecured.

5. Educate Yourself About Phishing Scams

Attackers often use fake login pages or email links to steal passwords. Always verify the URL of the Dropbox login page and avoid clicking on suspicious links.

Dropbox's Password Security Features

Dropbox actively monitors for compromised credentials and prompts users to reset passwords if they are found in breach datasets. The platform also restricts commonly used weak passwords to enhance security.

In Summary

Setting a strong password for your Dropbox account is a crucial step in securing your data. By adhering to best practices—using long, complex, and unique passwords, combined with regular updates and monitoring—you can ensure your account remains safe from malicious attacks.

Strong password management not only protects your Dropbox account but also contributes to better overall digital security practices in your personal and professional life.

5.1.3 Recognizing Suspicious Activity

Maintaining the security of your Dropbox account requires vigilance against suspicious activity. In today's digital landscape, cyberattacks and unauthorized account access are increasing in frequency and sophistication. This section provides actionable tips and best practices to help you identify and respond to any unusual behavior in your Dropbox account.

Understanding What Constitutes Suspicious Activity

Suspicious activity refers to any unauthorized or unusual action within your Dropbox account that may indicate a security threat. This includes but is not limited to:

- **Unexpected File Changes**: Files being edited, renamed, or deleted without your knowledge.
- **Unrecognized Devices or Locations**: Access attempts from devices or geographic regions that you don't recognize.
- **Unusual Sharing Activity**: Unauthorized sharing of files or folders with unknown individuals.
- **Unusual Login Attempts**: Frequent login attempts, especially from IP addresses in other countries.

Understanding these indicators is the first step to safeguarding your data.

Monitoring Account Activity

Dropbox provides built-in tools to help you monitor account activity effectively.

1. **Accessing the Security Dashboard**

    o   Log in to your Dropbox account on the web.

    o   Navigate to the **Security** section under your account settings.

    o   Review the **Devices** and **Web Sessions** tabs to see where your account is currently logged in.

    o   Check the **Account Activity Log** for recent actions like logins, file edits, or sharing.

2. **Reviewing Linked Devices**

    Ensure all linked devices are yours. If you notice any unrecognized devices, unlink them immediately and change your password.

3. **Setting Up Email Notifications**

    Dropbox can send email alerts for unusual activity, such as new logins from unknown devices or password changes. Enable this feature in your settings to stay informed.

Detecting Phishing Attempts

Phishing is one of the most common methods attackers use to gain unauthorized access to Dropbox accounts. Here's how to recognize and avoid phishing attempts:

- **Email Red Flags**: Be cautious of emails claiming to be from Dropbox that ask for sensitive information or contain links to external websites.

- **Fake Login Pages**: Verify that the URL in your browser's address bar is legitimate before entering your credentials. Dropbox's official domain is www.dropbox.com.

- **Unexpected File Requests**: Scammers may send file requests pretending to be a colleague or friend. Always confirm the sender's identity through another communication channel.

Responding to Unauthorized Access

If you suspect unauthorized access to your Dropbox account, follow these steps immediately:

1. **Change Your Password**
   - Use a strong, unique password. Avoid reusing passwords from other services.

2. **Enable Two-Factor Authentication (2FA)**
   - This adds an additional layer of security to your account, making it harder for attackers to gain access.

3. **Unlink Unauthorized Devices**
   - Go to the **Security** settings and unlink any unrecognized devices.

4. **Review Recent Activity**
   - Check your account activity log for unusual actions and report any suspicious activity to Dropbox Support.

Best Practices for Maintaining Vigilance

1. **Regularly Audit Your Account**
   - Periodically review your account settings, linked devices, and activity logs.
   - Update your password every few months to reduce risk.

2. **Educate Yourself and Your Team**
   - If you use Dropbox for business or team purposes, educate your team members about recognizing and reporting suspicious activity.

3. **Stay Updated on Security Threats**
   - Follow Dropbox's blog or security updates to stay informed about potential vulnerabilities or new security features.

Real-Life Examples

To better illustrate the importance of recognizing suspicious activity, consider these scenarios:

1. **Case Study: Unauthorized Access from Abroad**

    o   A user received an alert about a login attempt from a foreign country. Upon reviewing their security dashboard, they discovered an unrecognized device and quickly revoked access, preventing data loss.

2. **Phishing Attack Prevention**

    o   A Dropbox user received an email claiming their account was about to be suspended. Recognizing the misspelled URL in the link, they reported the email as phishing and avoided compromising their credentials.

Dropbox's Role in Assisting Users

Dropbox actively works to protect its users from threats:

- **Fraud Detection Algorithms**: Dropbox monitors accounts for unusual activity patterns and alerts users if anomalies are detected.

- **Support for Victims**: Dropbox's support team assists users who suspect unauthorized access or account breaches.

Conclusion

Recognizing suspicious activity in your Dropbox account is an essential skill for maintaining the security of your data. By understanding the warning signs, utilizing Dropbox's security tools, and practicing vigilance, you can minimize the risk of unauthorized access. Remember, the security of your account is a shared responsibility between you and Dropbox. Stay proactive to ensure your data remains safe.

5.2 Managing Permissions and Access

Managing permissions and access in Dropbox is a critical aspect of ensuring that your data is shared securely. Dropbox provides robust tools for granting and controlling access to your files and folders, enabling you to share content while retaining control over who can view, edit, or manage your information. This section focuses on sharing files and folders with limited access, offering practical guidance on how to use Dropbox's features effectively.

5.2.1 Sharing with Limited Access

Sharing with limited access in Dropbox allows you to provide specific individuals or groups with restricted permissions to view or edit your files and folders. This feature is essential for maintaining security while collaborating with others. Here's how you can set up and manage limited access sharing:

Understanding Sharing Permissions

Dropbox offers three primary levels of permissions:

1. **View-Only Access**: Users can see and download the files but cannot make changes.

2. **Edit Access**: Users can modify the content, rename files, or move items within the shared folder.

3. **Owner Access**: This permission level is exclusive to the person who created the file or folder, allowing them to manage all aspects of access and permissions.

Before sharing a file or folder, it's crucial to determine the level of access required by the recipient. For example, if you're collaborating on a document with a colleague, edit access may be appropriate. However, if you're sharing a finalized report with a client, view-only access is typically sufficient.

How to Share with Limited Access

1. **Via Dropbox Web**:
    - Navigate to the file or folder you want to share.
    - Click the **Share** button next to the file or folder name.
    - Enter the email addresses of the people you want to share with.
    - Use the dropdown menu next to their names to select the desired permission level: "Can View" or "Can Edit."
    - Add an optional message explaining the purpose of the shared file.
    - Click **Share** to finalize.

2. **Using the Dropbox Desktop App**:
    - Open your Dropbox folder on your computer.
    - Right-click the file or folder and select **Share**.
    - Follow the same steps as above to set permissions and invite collaborators.

3. **On Mobile Devices**:
    - Open the Dropbox app and locate the file or folder.
    - Tap the three-dot menu and select **Share**.
    - Add the recipient's email, choose permissions, and send the invitation.

Advanced Sharing Options

Dropbox provides additional features to fine-tune sharing permissions:

1. **Password-Protected Links**: For sensitive files, you can generate a shared link and set a password, ensuring only authorized individuals can access the content.

2. **Expiration Dates for Links**: When sharing temporary files, set an expiration date for the link to ensure it becomes inaccessible after a specified time.

3. **Restricting Downloads**: For view-only access, you can disable the download option, allowing recipients to view the file online without saving a local copy.

Use Cases for Limited Access

- **Personal Sharing**: Share photos or documents with family members, granting view-only access to prevent accidental edits.

- **Business Collaboration**: Provide edit access to team members working on a shared project while restricting others to view-only.

- **Client Deliverables**: Share final project deliverables with clients using view-only links and optional password protection.

Best Practices for Secure Sharing

To maximize security and minimize risks when sharing with limited access, follow these best practices:

1. **Regularly Review Permissions**: Periodically check who has access to your files and update permissions as needed.

2. **Use Unique Links for Different Recipients**: If you're sharing the same file with multiple people, create unique links with tailored permissions for better control.

3. **Enable Notifications**: Set up notifications to stay informed when someone accesses or edits a shared file.

4. **Audit Activity Logs**: Use Dropbox's activity logs to monitor file access and identify any unauthorized changes or downloads.

Common Pitfalls and How to Avoid Them

1. **Over-Sharing Permissions**: Avoid giving edit access to users who only need to view files.

2. **Neglecting to Remove Old Access**: After a project ends, revoke access for collaborators who no longer need it.

3. **Sharing Without Passwords**: Always use password protection for sensitive files shared with external parties.

Frequently Asked Questions (FAQs)

Q1: Can I restrict access to specific subfolders within a shared folder?
Yes, Dropbox allows you to share subfolders separately, granting unique permissions for each subfolder.

Q2: What happens if I revoke someone's access to a file they have downloaded?
Revoking access only affects their ability to view or edit the file online; downloaded copies remain accessible unless manually deleted.

Q3: Is there a limit to the number of people I can share a file with?
There is no strict limit, but sharing with a large number of users may require a Dropbox Business or Team account for better management.

Conclusion

Sharing with limited access in Dropbox is a powerful way to balance collaboration and security. By understanding permission levels, utilizing advanced sharing options, and adhering to best practices, you can ensure your files remain safe while fostering effective teamwork. In the next section, we'll explore how to revoke or adjust permissions to maintain control over your shared content.

5.2.2 Revoking Access from Users

Managing permissions and controlling who can access your files and folders is crucial to ensuring the security and integrity of your data. Dropbox makes it simple to revoke access from users, whether they are individuals who no longer require access or unauthorized users who pose a security risk. This section will guide you through the process of revoking access from users in various scenarios and provide best practices to maintain secure collaboration.

Understanding the Importance of Revoking Access

Revoking access is essential for several reasons:

- **Preventing Unauthorized Use:** Removing access from users who are no longer involved ensures that your files cannot be misused.

- **Maintaining Confidentiality:** Sensitive information should only be accessible to those who need it.

- **Improving Collaboration Management:** Keeping access lists up-to-date avoids confusion about who has permission to view or edit shared files.

Regularly reviewing and managing permissions is a proactive step in maintaining the security of your Dropbox workspace.

When Should You Revoke Access?

Here are some common situations where revoking access becomes necessary:

- **User Has Left the Organization:** When an employee, freelancer, or contractor leaves your team.

- **Project Completion:** Once a project is finished, access to related folders may no longer be needed.

- **Accidental Sharing:** If you mistakenly shared a file or folder with the wrong person.

- **Compromised Accounts:** If you suspect a user's account has been compromised.

- **Policy Changes:** Organizational policies might require restricting access to certain sensitive data.

Being vigilant in these scenarios helps protect your data and prevent potential issues.

Steps to Revoke Access from Users in Dropbox

Revoking access depends on the type of sharing you've used (link sharing or folder permissions) and the platform you're using. Here's a step-by-step guide for different methods:

1. Revoking Access to Shared Folders

If you've shared a folder with specific users and want to remove their access:

- **On the Web Interface:**
    1. Log in to your Dropbox account.
    2. Navigate to the **Shared** section from the left-hand menu.
    3. Select the folder for which you want to revoke access.
    4. Click the **'Share'** button next to the folder.
    5. In the pop-up, find the user whose access you wish to revoke.
    6. Click the dropdown menu next to their name and select **'Remove'**.
    7. Confirm your action when prompted.

- **On the Mobile App:**
    1. Open the Dropbox app on your device.
    2. Go to the **Shared** tab.
    3. Locate the folder in question and tap the '...' (more options) icon.
    4. Select **Manage Access** or **Share Settings**.
    5. Identify the user and tap **'Remove Access'**.

Once access is revoked, the user will no longer see the folder in their Dropbox account. However, any previously downloaded files on their device will remain unless manually deleted.

2. Revoking Access to Shared Links

If you've shared a file or folder via a link, you can disable the link to prevent further access:

- **On the Web Interface:**
    1. Go to the **Shared** section in your Dropbox account.
    2. Locate the file or folder with an active shared link.

3. Click the **'Share'** button.

4. Under the link-sharing options, select **'Disable Link'** or **'Remove Link'**.

- **On the Mobile App:**

    1. Open the file or folder with a shared link.

    2. Tap the '...' (more options) icon.

    3. Select **Manage Access** or **Link Settings**.

    4. Turn off the link sharing toggle.

This action makes the shared link inaccessible to anyone who tries to use it.

3. Managing Team Accounts and Permissions

For Dropbox Business or Team accounts, administrators have enhanced controls:

- **From the Admin Console:**

    1. Log in as the admin to your team's Dropbox account.

    2. Navigate to the **Admin Console** and select **Members**.

    3. Identify the user whose access you want to revoke.

    4. Click on their name, then choose **'Sign Out of All Sessions'** to immediately disconnect them from the account.

    5. If necessary, remove their membership from specific team folders or suspend their account entirely.

Removing a user from a team account ensures they lose access to all shared folders and resources tied to the organization.

Best Practices for Revoking Access

To maximize security and minimize disruptions, follow these best practices:

1. **Regular Access Reviews:** Periodically audit the list of users with access to your folders and files.

2. **Clear Communication:** Inform collaborators when their access will be revoked, especially in professional or team settings.

3. **Use Expiring Links:** For temporary sharing, Dropbox allows you to set expiration dates for shared links, automatically revoking access after a specific period.

4. **Monitor Activity Logs:** For Dropbox Business users, the Activity Logs feature helps track changes and identify unauthorized access.

5. **Document Access Changes:** Maintain records of who has been granted or revoked access, especially for sensitive projects.

What Happens After Revoking Access?

When you revoke access:

- **Immediate Disconnection:** The user can no longer view or edit the file or folder.

- **No Notification (By Default):** Dropbox does not notify the user that their access has been revoked unless you manually inform them.

- **Offline Files Remain:** If the user has downloaded files locally, those copies remain on their device unless deleted.

To ensure complete security, ask collaborators to delete local copies of files they no longer need access to.

Troubleshooting Issues with Revoking Access

If you encounter difficulties while revoking access:

- **User Not Found:** Double-check that the user is listed as a collaborator. They may have accessed the file via a shared link rather than direct folder access.

- **Persistent Access:** If a user still appears to have access, confirm that you've removed all associated permissions, including shared links and subfolder permissions.

- **Revoked But Still Visible:** Revoked folders may remain visible on a user's account for a short time. This typically resolves within a few minutes.

Revoking access is a critical part of managing permissions in Dropbox, ensuring that your files are secure while enabling effective collaboration. With these tools and strategies, you can confidently control who has access to your shared resources.

5.2.3 Adjusting Team Permissions

Effectively managing team permissions is essential for maintaining security and ensuring smooth collaboration in a shared Dropbox environment. Dropbox provides robust tools to allow admins and team members to manage permissions with precision, giving the right people access to the right files while protecting sensitive information. In this section, we'll explore the process of adjusting team permissions, highlighting best practices to optimize team functionality.

Understanding Team Permissions in Dropbox

Team permissions are hierarchical settings that control how users within a team can interact with shared content. Dropbox differentiates permissions at various levels:

1. **Folder-Level Permissions**: These permissions dictate who can view, edit, or manage specific folders within the team.

2. **Role-Based Permissions**: Team members may have roles such as Admin, Editor, or Viewer, each with varying degrees of access and responsibility.

3. **File-Level Permissions**: Individual files within shared folders can have unique access settings for added granularity.

By combining these layers, Dropbox enables detailed control over content distribution and access, ensuring team members have only the permissions they need to perform their tasks.

Steps to Adjust Team Permissions

1. **Accessing the Admin Console**

- Navigate to the **Admin Console** from the Dropbox dashboard.
- Select the **Content** tab to view a list of shared folders and files within the team.

2. **Identifying the Folder or File to Adjust**
    - Locate the folder or file for which you wish to modify permissions.
    - Use the search function or browse through the directory tree for easy navigation.

3. **Setting Permissions at the Folder Level**
    - Click on the folder and select **Share** from the options.
    - Review the current permissions. For each team member, choose between:
        - **Viewer**: Can only view files.
        - **Editor**: Can view and modify files.
        - **Owner**: Has full control, including the ability to manage access.

4. **Adjusting Permissions for Subfolders or Files**
    - Expand the folder to display subfolders or files.
    - Assign permissions individually if required. This is useful for restricting access to sensitive data within a broader folder.

5. **Modifying Role-Based Permissions**
    - In the Admin Console, go to the **Members** tab.
    - Select a team member and adjust their role. Options include:
        - **Team Admin**: Full administrative privileges over the account.
        - **Support Admin**: Limited admin privileges for support-related tasks.
        - **Team Member**: Standard user access.

6. **Reconfirming Changes**

- o Always double-check your changes. Ensure that permissions align with your team's operational needs and security policies.

Best Practices for Adjusting Team Permissions

1. Apply the Principle of Least Privilege (PoLP)

Grant the minimum permissions necessary for team members to perform their roles. This reduces the risk of accidental data leaks and unauthorized access.

2. Use Role-Based Access Control (RBAC)

Assign team members roles based on their responsibilities. For example, Admins should have broad access, while entry-level members should only access what's necessary for their tasks.

3. Regularly Audit Permissions

Perform periodic reviews of team permissions to ensure they remain relevant as roles and projects evolve. Remove access for team members who are no longer part of a project.

4. Communicate Permission Policies

Clearly communicate permission policies to all team members. Educate them about their roles and responsibilities to minimize misuse or confusion.

Common Scenarios for Adjusting Permissions

Scenario 1: Onboarding a New Team Member

When a new member joins, assign them a role based on their position. For instance, a marketing team member may only need access to shared marketing materials, not financial data.

Scenario 2: Collaborating with External Contractors

If an external contractor requires access to specific files, grant them Viewer or Editor permissions for the relevant folders. Limit their access duration by setting an expiration date for the shared link.

Scenario 3: Transitioning Roles

When a team member transitions to a new role, update their permissions to reflect their new responsibilities. This often involves revoking access to previous projects and granting access to new ones.

Leveraging Dropbox Tools for Permission Management

Dropbox offers several advanced features to streamline permission management:

1. **Link Sharing Settings**
   Control link sharing by setting permissions such as:

   - View only.
   - Edit access.
   - Password protection or expiration dates for links.

2. **Activity Monitoring**

   Use activity logs to track changes in permissions and detect unauthorized modifications.

3. **Team Folders**

   Team folders allow centralized permission management for large groups. Adjusting permissions at the team folder level automatically cascades to all subfolders and files.

Troubleshooting Permission Issues

Problem 1: A Team Member Can't Access a Folder

- Solution: Verify that they have been granted the correct level of access. Ensure they are part of the shared folder or team.

Problem 2: A Former Member Still Has Access

- Solution: Revoke their access from the Admin Console immediately. For additional security, reset sharing links.

Problem 3: Conflicting Permissions

- Solution: Review the folder hierarchy to identify overlapping settings. Always prioritize higher-level permissions for resolution.

Conclusion

Adjusting team permissions is a critical aspect of managing a secure and productive Dropbox environment. By carefully assigning roles and access levels, you can foster efficient collaboration while protecting sensitive data. Leveraging Dropbox's permission management tools and adhering to best practices ensures your team can work seamlessly, even in complex shared environments.

5.3 Data Privacy

5.3.1 Understanding Dropbox's Privacy Policy

Privacy is a fundamental concern for individuals and businesses when storing and sharing files in the cloud. Dropbox, as one of the leading cloud storage providers, has implemented robust privacy measures and policies to safeguard user data. This section explains Dropbox's Privacy Policy in detail, highlighting its key aspects and what they mean for you as a user.

What Is the Dropbox Privacy Policy?

The Dropbox Privacy Policy outlines how the company collects, uses, and protects your personal information. It provides transparency about what data is stored, how it is processed, and the steps Dropbox takes to ensure the security of your files and personal details. Understanding this policy is crucial for making informed decisions about your data management practices.

Data Collection Practices

Dropbox collects data to provide its services, improve functionality, and enhance user experience. The main categories of data collected include:

1. **Account Information**
   - **What is collected:** Your name, email address, and payment details (if applicable).
   - **Why it's collected:** This information is required for account creation, billing, and communication purposes.

2. **Usage Data**
   - **What is collected:** Information about how you interact with Dropbox, such as the features you use, the files you upload, and the devices you connect.

- **Why it's collected:** This helps Dropbox optimize its platform and tailor features to better meet user needs.

3. **Device Information**

    - **What is collected:** Device type, operating system, IP address, and browser information.

    - **Why it's collected:** This data enhances security by identifying unauthorized access and supports troubleshooting efforts.

4. **Cookies and Tracking Technologies**

    - **What is collected:** Cookies and similar technologies track user preferences and activity on the website and app.

    - **Why it's collected:** This ensures a seamless experience, such as remembering login credentials or saving preferred settings.

How Dropbox Uses Your Data

Dropbox uses the collected data to deliver its services effectively. The key purposes include:

1. **Providing Core Services**

    - Syncing and storing files securely.

    - Facilitating file sharing and collaboration.

2. **Improving Product Features**

    - Analyzing usage trends to introduce new tools and functionalities.

    - Refining existing features for better user experience.

3. **Enhancing Security**

    - Monitoring for suspicious activity.

    - Implementing measures to prevent unauthorized access.

4. **Marketing and Communication**

    - Sending updates, promotional offers, and service-related notifications.

Dropbox's Data Sharing Practices

Dropbox emphasizes limited and responsible data sharing. Here's how and when your data might be shared:

1. **With Third-Party Vendors**

    o   Dropbox partners with vendors to provide services such as payment processing, customer support, and data analytics. These vendors are bound by confidentiality agreements and only access data necessary to perform their roles.

2. **With Other Users**

    o   When you share files or collaborate on documents, your data (like email addresses or shared content) becomes visible to the intended recipients.

3. **For Legal Compliance**

    o   Dropbox may disclose information to comply with legal obligations, such as court orders or government requests.

4. **During Business Transfers**

    o   In the event of mergers or acquisitions, your data may be transferred as part of business assets. Dropbox ensures that privacy standards are upheld during such transitions.

Data Protection Measures

Dropbox employs several mechanisms to protect your data against breaches and unauthorized access. These include:

1. **Encryption**

    o   Files are encrypted both in transit (using SSL/TLS protocols) and at rest (using AES-256 encryption). This ensures that your data remains unreadable to unauthorized parties.

2. **Access Controls**

- Dropbox restricts employee access to user data unless necessary for troubleshooting or maintenance.

3. **Regular Security Audits**

    - The company conducts regular audits and vulnerability testing to identify and mitigate potential threats.

4. **Compliance with Standards**

    - Dropbox adheres to industry regulations such as GDPR (General Data Protection Regulation) and HIPAA (Health Insurance Portability and Accountability Act), ensuring compliance with strict privacy laws.

Your Privacy Rights

Dropbox recognizes the importance of empowering users to control their data. Here's what you can do to manage your privacy:

1. **Access Your Data**

    - You can request a copy of the information Dropbox stores about you.

2. **Update or Delete Data**

    - Update personal details through account settings or permanently delete your account to remove stored data.

3. **Opt-Out of Marketing Communications**

    - Adjust preferences to stop receiving promotional emails.

4. **Configure Sharing Settings**

    - Control who can view or edit shared files and folders.

Frequently Asked Questions About Privacy

1. **Can Dropbox employees access my files?**

- Dropbox employees do not access user files unless necessary for technical reasons or under legal obligations. All such actions are logged and monitored.

2. **What happens to my data if I stop using Dropbox?**
    - Your files remain accessible until you delete them. Deleted accounts and files are permanently erased after a specified retention period.

3. **How secure are shared links?**
    - Shared links are protected but can be made more secure by enabling passwords and expiration dates.

4. **Does Dropbox sell my data to advertisers?**
    - No, Dropbox does not sell user data to third parties.

Conclusion

Understanding Dropbox's Privacy Policy empowers you to make informed decisions about how you use the platform. By knowing what data is collected, how it's used, and the measures in place to protect it, you can trust Dropbox as a secure and reliable cloud storage solution.

5.3.2 Tips for Protecting Your Data

In today's digital age, protecting your data has become more critical than ever. Dropbox provides robust security features to safeguard your files, but users must also take proactive steps to ensure the highest level of protection. This section outlines practical tips and best practices for keeping your data safe while using Dropbox.

Understand the Basics of Data Protection

Before diving into specific tips, it's essential to understand why data protection is necessary. Cyber threats, accidental deletions, or unauthorized access can compromise your files, leading to financial losses or reputational damage. Taking preventative measures not only secures your data but also provides peace of mind.

1. Secure Your Account with Strong Credentials

Your Dropbox account is the gateway to your data. Securing it begins with a strong password:

- **Create a Unique Password**: Avoid using the same password for multiple accounts. A strong password should include a combination of uppercase and lowercase letters, numbers, and special characters.

- **Avoid Predictable Passwords**: Steer clear of commonly used phrases, such as "123456" or "password." Consider using a passphrase like "SecureMyData2024!" for added security.

- **Use a Password Manager**: If remembering complex passwords is challenging, use a trusted password manager to generate and store them securely.

2. Enable Two-Factor Authentication (2FA)

Two-factor authentication adds an additional layer of security. Even if someone obtains your password, they'll need a second authentication factor (e.g., a code sent to your phone). Here's how to enable 2FA in Dropbox:

- Navigate to your account settings and select the **Security** tab.

- Choose **Enable Two-Factor Authentication** and follow the prompts to set up SMS or an authentication app like Google Authenticator.

- Regularly update your 2FA settings to ensure the registered phone number or app is current.

3. Monitor Account Activity Regularly

Dropbox provides tools to review and monitor account activity. These tools help you spot suspicious activities before they escalate.

- **Review Recent Login History**: Check for any unauthorized access by visiting the security section of your account.

- **Track Shared Links**: Regularly review the files and folders you've shared to ensure they are still relevant and secure.

- **Set Alerts**: Enable email notifications for account logins from unrecognized devices.

4. Limit Access to Sensitive Files

Be mindful of who can view or edit your files. Use Dropbox's sharing permissions to control access:

- **Set View-Only Permissions**: If someone doesn't need to edit a file, set their access to "view-only."

- **Use Password-Protected Links**: For particularly sensitive files, enable password protection for shared links.

- **Set Expiration Dates for Shared Links**: Ensure that access to your files doesn't remain open indefinitely.

5. Encrypt Sensitive Files Before Uploading

For an added layer of protection, consider encrypting sensitive files before uploading them to Dropbox. While Dropbox uses encryption to protect data during transfer and at rest, encrypting files yourself adds another layer of security.

- **Use Encryption Software**: Tools like VeraCrypt or AxCrypt are excellent for encrypting files.

- **Securely Store Encryption Keys**: Keep the keys or passwords used for encryption in a safe place, such as a password manager.

6. Keep Your Devices Secure

Data protection isn't just about online security; your devices also play a role.

- **Install Antivirus Software**: Ensure your devices are free from malware that could compromise your Dropbox files.

- **Enable Device Lock**: Use passwords, PINs, or biometric authentication to lock your devices.

- **Log Out from Unused Devices**: If you no longer use a device, log out of Dropbox to prevent unauthorized access.

7. Regularly Back Up Your Data

Even with Dropbox's robust storage and recovery features, it's wise to maintain a separate backup of critical files.

- **Use an External Drive**: Periodically download important files to an external hard drive or USB.

- **Sync with Another Cloud Service**: Consider using an additional cloud storage service as a secondary backup.

8. Stay Updated on Dropbox Security Features

Dropbox frequently updates its platform with new security features. Staying informed ensures you can take full advantage of these updates.

- **Read Security Announcements**: Subscribe to Dropbox's newsletters or blog for updates.

- **Participate in Beta Features**: Early access to security enhancements can keep your account safer.

9. Educate Yourself About Phishing Attacks

Phishing is a common method attackers use to steal credentials. Dropbox users should be vigilant about emails or messages that seem suspicious.

- **Verify Email Senders**: Check the sender's email address for authenticity. Dropbox emails typically come from "@dropbox.com."

- **Avoid Clicking on Unverified Links**: Hover over links to check their destination before clicking.
- **Report Phishing Attempts**: Notify Dropbox if you receive suspicious messages claiming to be from them.

10. Use Advanced Security Tools for Business Accounts

If you're a Dropbox Business user, you have access to additional security tools:

- **Admin Controls**: Set organization-wide policies for file sharing and permissions.
- **Team Activity Monitoring**: Use the admin dashboard to track how team members use Dropbox.
- **Integrate with Security Platforms**: Dropbox supports integration with advanced security tools like single sign-on (SSO) and data loss prevention (DLP) systems.

Final Thoughts

Protecting your data on Dropbox involves a combination of using the platform's built-in security features and adopting good personal security practices. By following the tips in this section, you can significantly reduce the risk of unauthorized access and ensure your data remains safe and secure.

5.3.3 Handling Compliance Requirements

As organizations increasingly rely on cloud storage solutions like Dropbox, ensuring compliance with various legal, regulatory, and industry standards becomes a critical aspect of data management. Whether you're a business user or an individual handling sensitive information, adhering to compliance requirements is essential for avoiding penalties and maintaining trust.

Understanding Compliance in the Context of Dropbox

Compliance refers to adhering to the rules, regulations, and standards relevant to your industry or jurisdiction. These requirements may include data protection laws such as the **General Data Protection Regulation (GDPR)** in the European Union, the **Health Insurance Portability and Accountability Act (HIPAA)** in the United States, or other regional data privacy laws like **CCPA** (California Consumer Privacy Act). Dropbox provides tools and features to help users align their file storage and sharing practices with such regulations.

Why Compliance Matters

1. **Legal and Financial Consequences:** Non-compliance can lead to significant fines and legal actions.

2. **Reputation Management:** Mishandling sensitive information can damage trust among clients, partners, or stakeholders.

3. **Operational Efficiency:** Meeting compliance standards helps streamline data management and enhances operational workflows.

Dropbox is built with security and compliance at its core, offering features designed to meet the needs of various industries.

Steps to Handle Compliance Requirements with Dropbox

1. Identify Relevant Regulations

Before using Dropbox for data storage, understand the compliance standards applicable to your use case. For example:

- If you handle personal data of EU residents, GDPR compliance is mandatory.
- For healthcare organizations in the U.S., HIPAA applies.
- Businesses in financial services might need to follow standards such as PCI DSS (Payment Card Industry Data Security Standard).

Work with legal advisors or compliance officers to map out the requirements specific to your organization.

2. Use Dropbox Business Plans with Compliance Features

Dropbox offers specific plans tailored to help organizations meet compliance standards:

- **Dropbox Business Advanced:** Features include advanced security controls, audit logs, and device management tools.
- **Dropbox Enterprise:** Includes additional tools for managing compliance across large teams, with dedicated support for regulatory concerns.

Both plans are designed to assist users in maintaining compliance with data privacy and security laws.

3. Leverage Admin Controls and Audit Tools

Dropbox's admin controls allow organizations to monitor and manage data access, ensuring compliance with policies:

- **Activity Logs:** Track who accessed or edited files and folders.
- **Permission Settings:** Grant access only to authorized personnel.
- **Data Classification:** Use metadata and tags to categorize files by sensitivity or compliance needs.

These tools help ensure that sensitive data is stored and shared appropriately, minimizing the risk of breaches.

Key Dropbox Features for Compliance

1. Data Encryption

Dropbox encrypts data at rest and in transit using advanced protocols, such as AES-256 and TLS, ensuring that information is protected from unauthorized access.

2. Geographic Data Hosting Options

To comply with regional data protection laws, Dropbox allows businesses to store data in specific geographic regions. This feature is particularly helpful for GDPR compliance, as it ensures that data remains within the EU.

3. Access Controls and Authentication

Dropbox's role-based access controls ensure that only authorized users can view or modify files. Multi-factor authentication adds an additional layer of security, critical for compliance.

Handling Specific Compliance Scenarios

1. GDPR Compliance

Under GDPR, organizations are required to:

- **Obtain Consent:** Ensure individuals have given explicit permission for their data to be processed.
- **Provide Transparency:** Inform users about how their data will be used.
- **Ensure Data Portability:** Allow users to access and transfer their data upon request.

Dropbox supports GDPR compliance with features like data export tools, audit logs, and clear privacy policies.

2. HIPAA Compliance

Healthcare organizations in the U.S. can use Dropbox for HIPAA-compliant file storage and sharing if they sign a **Business Associate Agreement (BAA)** with Dropbox. Key features include:

- **Secure File Sharing:** Limit access to only authorized personnel.
- **Data Retention Policies:** Ensure sensitive information is retained only as long as required by law.
- **Encryption Standards:** Safeguard patient records during storage and transfer.

3. PCI DSS Compliance

For businesses handling payment information, Dropbox facilitates compliance by securing payment card data through encryption and robust access controls. While Dropbox itself does not process payments, it can securely store documents related to financial transactions.

Creating a Culture of Compliance

Compliance is not just about using the right tools; it's also about fostering awareness and accountability:

1. **Employee Training:** Educate team members on compliance best practices and how to use Dropbox's security features effectively.

2. **Regular Audits:** Schedule periodic audits to ensure that your Dropbox usage aligns with the latest regulations.

3. **Policy Development:** Draft and enforce policies on acceptable data storage and sharing practices within Dropbox.

Dropbox provides resources and support to help organizations create a compliance-focused environment.

Staying Ahead of Regulatory Changes

Laws and standards evolve over time, and it's crucial to stay updated:

- Subscribe to legal and regulatory updates in your industry.

- Regularly review Dropbox's compliance-related features, as new tools are often introduced to address emerging needs.

- Engage with Dropbox's customer support for guidance on meeting new compliance requirements.

By maintaining a proactive approach, you can ensure ongoing alignment with compliance standards while using Dropbox.

Conclusion

Handling compliance requirements may seem daunting, but Dropbox simplifies the process by offering secure, scalable, and compliant cloud storage solutions. By understanding the regulations applicable to your data and leveraging Dropbox's powerful features, you can protect sensitive information, build trust, and avoid costly penalties. Whether you're an individual user or a business, ensuring compliance is a vital step in using Dropbox responsibly and effectively.

CHAPTER VI
Troubleshooting and FAQs

6.1 Common Issues and Solutions

6.1.1 Sync Problems

Dropbox sync issues can be frustrating, especially when you rely on the platform to ensure your files are up-to-date across all devices. This section will walk you through common sync problems and provide practical solutions to get everything back on track.

What Are Sync Problems in Dropbox?

Sync problems occur when files or folders fail to upload, download, or update across devices as expected. These issues can lead to discrepancies between what's on your local device and what's stored in your Dropbox account. Some common indicators of sync problems include:

- Files that are stuck uploading or downloading.
- A missing green checkmark indicating sync completion.
- Outdated file versions on one or more devices.

Common Causes of Sync Problems

Several factors can disrupt the sync process in Dropbox. Understanding these causes is the first step to resolving them:

1. **Poor or Unstable Internet Connection:** A weak connection can hinder Dropbox's ability to upload or download files effectively.

2. **Conflicting File Names:** Files with unsupported characters or duplicate names can create conflicts during sync.

3. **Outdated Dropbox App:** Running an older version of Dropbox may lead to compatibility issues.

4. **Limited Disk Space:** If your device runs out of storage, Dropbox may struggle to sync files.

5. **Paused Syncing:** Users might accidentally pause syncing, halting the upload and download processes.

6. **Selective Sync Settings:** If certain folders are excluded from sync, files in those folders won't appear on other devices.

7. **File Permissions:** Lack of proper permissions can prevent Dropbox from accessing or modifying files.

Step-by-Step Solutions to Sync Problems

1. Check Your Internet Connection

- Ensure your device is connected to a stable network.
- If using Wi-Fi, try restarting your router or switching to a wired connection.
- Test your connection speed to verify it meets Dropbox's requirements for syncing large files.

2. Verify Sync Status

Dropbox provides visual cues for sync status:

- **Green checkmark:** Sync complete.
- **Blue circle with arrows:** Sync in progress.
- **Red X:** Sync error.

If you see a red X or no sync icon, open the Dropbox desktop app and check the sync status in the settings menu.

3. Resolve File Name Conflicts

- Rename files to remove unsupported characters (e.g., <, >, :, ", ?, *, |).
- Avoid excessively long file names or paths exceeding 260 characters.
- Use unique names to prevent duplication conflicts.

4. Update the Dropbox App

- Open the Dropbox app and check for updates.
- Download and install the latest version from the Dropbox website.
- Restart the app after updating to ensure proper installation.

5. Ensure Sufficient Storage Space

- Verify the available disk space on your device.
    - On Windows: Check via File Explorer > This PC.
    - On macOS: Click the Apple menu > About This Mac > Storage.
- Delete unnecessary files to free up space.

6. Review Selective Sync Settings

- Open the Dropbox app on your desktop.
- Go to Preferences > Sync > Selective Sync.
- Ensure the folders you need are selected for syncing.

7. Reauthorize Your Account

Sometimes, signing out and back into your Dropbox account can resolve authentication issues:

- Click your profile picture in the Dropbox app.
- Select "Sign Out" and restart the app.
- Log back in using your credentials.

8. Grant Necessary Permissions

- On Windows: Right-click the Dropbox folder > Properties > Security tab > Edit permissions.

- On macOS: Right-click the Dropbox folder > Get Info > Sharing & Permissions.

Additional Tools for Diagnosing Sync Issues

Dropbox Sync Icons

Dropbox uses icons to provide real-time feedback on file status. If you encounter an issue, refer to these indicators:

- **Gray minus sign:** File excluded via Selective Sync.
- **Red X:** File failed to sync.
- **Gray cloud icon:** File is online-only.

Activity Logs

The Dropbox desktop app logs recent activity to help diagnose sync problems:

- Open the app and click your profile picture.
- Select "View Sync Issues" to see a detailed report.

When to Contact Dropbox Support

If you've tried the above solutions and your sync issues persist, consider reaching out to Dropbox support:

1. Visit the Help Center.
2. Submit a support ticket with details about your issue.
3. Include screenshots of error messages or sync icons for faster resolution.

Preventing Future Sync Problems

1. **Maintain a Stable Internet Connection:** Use a reliable network, especially when syncing large files.
2. **Regularly Update Dropbox:** Enable auto-updates to ensure you're always using the latest version.

3. **Organize Files Effectively:** Keep file names short, unique, and free from special characters.

4. **Monitor Disk Space:** Periodically check your device's storage capacity to avoid running out of space.

5. **Backup Important Data:** Use Dropbox's backup feature or an external drive as a failsafe.

By understanding the root causes of sync problems and following these troubleshooting steps, you can resolve issues quickly and ensure seamless operation of your Dropbox account. With these tips, you'll be able to keep your files accessible and up-to-date across all your devices.

6.1.2 Login Issues

Dropbox is designed to provide seamless access to your files from anywhere, but sometimes users may encounter login issues that disrupt their experience. These problems can stem from various causes, ranging from simple user errors to technical difficulties. This section explores common login issues, their causes, and step-by-step solutions to help you regain access quickly.

1. Forgotten Passwords

Forgetting your password is a common issue, but Dropbox makes it easy to reset your credentials.

Solution:

1. Navigate to the Dropbox login page.

2. Click the **"Forgot your password?"** link below the password field.

3. Enter the email address associated with your Dropbox account.

4. Check your inbox for a password reset email from Dropbox. (Ensure you check your spam folder if you don't see the email in your main inbox.)

5. Click the link in the email and follow the instructions to create a new password.
6. Log in to your account using the new password.

Tips to Avoid This Issue in the Future:

- Use a password manager to securely store your login credentials.
- Create a memorable password that combines uppercase letters, lowercase letters, numbers, and symbols.

2. Incorrect Email or Password

Users sometimes mistype their email or password, which can prevent successful login attempts.

Solution:

1. Double-check that you are entering the correct email address associated with your account.
2. Verify the password is typed correctly. Be mindful of capitalization, as Dropbox passwords are case-sensitive.
3. If you suspect your email or password has been compromised, reset your password using the steps outlined above.

3. Account Locked Due to Suspicious Activity

Dropbox may lock your account temporarily if it detects unusual login attempts or suspicious activity to protect your data.

Solution:

1. Look for an email from Dropbox explaining the reason for the account lock.
2. Follow the instructions provided in the email to verify your identity. This may involve entering a verification code sent to your registered email or phone number.
3. If you can't find the email or access your account, contact Dropbox Support for assistance.

Preventive Measures:

- Enable two-factor authentication (2FA) for an added layer of security.
- Avoid using public Wi-Fi when accessing your Dropbox account, as this can increase the risk of unauthorized access.

4. Two-Factor Authentication (2FA) Issues

While 2FA adds security, it can occasionally cause login problems if you lose access to your phone or authenticator app.

Solution:

1. Use your backup codes provided when you first enabled 2FA. These codes can be used to log in without the need for a 2FA device.
2. If you no longer have your backup codes, contact Dropbox Support to verify your identity and regain access.
3. Once you regain access, update your 2FA settings to ensure future login attempts are smooth.

Best Practices for 2FA Management:

- Store your backup codes in a secure location, such as a password manager.
- If you upgrade to a new phone, transfer your authenticator app data before resetting your old device.

5. Browser and App Compatibility Issues

Login attempts can fail if your browser or Dropbox app is not updated or is incompatible with the platform.

Solution:

1. Clear your browser cache and cookies, as outdated data can interfere with login processes.
2. Update your browser or Dropbox app to the latest version.

3. Try accessing your account using a different browser or device to identify whether the issue is specific to your current setup.

Recommended Browsers and Devices:

- Dropbox works best with popular browsers like Google Chrome, Mozilla Firefox, and Microsoft Edge.

- Ensure your operating system (Windows, macOS, Android, or iOS) is updated for optimal compatibility.

6. Email Verification Issues

New users may struggle to log in if they haven't verified their email address.

Solution:

1. Check your inbox for a verification email from Dropbox.

2. Click the link in the email to verify your email address.

3. If you didn't receive the email, click the "Resend verification email" option on the login page.

4. Confirm that your email provider is not blocking emails from Dropbox. Add Dropbox to your email's "safe sender" list if necessary.

7. Multiple Accounts Confusion

Having multiple Dropbox accounts can lead to login errors if you mistakenly use the wrong credentials.

Solution:

1. Determine which email address is associated with the account you are trying to access.

2. Log out of all accounts on your device to ensure you start fresh.

3. Use the correct credentials for the desired account.

4. If you use multiple accounts frequently, consider linking them within Dropbox to switch between accounts more easily.

8. Network Connectivity Issues

A weak or unstable internet connection can also cause login problems.

Solution:

1. Check your internet connection and ensure it is stable.
2. Restart your router or switch to a different network if needed.
3. Disable any VPNs or proxy servers that might interfere with Dropbox's login system.

Testing Your Connection:

- Open a browser and navigate to another website to confirm your internet is working.
- Use Dropbox's connection test tool (available in the Help Center) to diagnose specific network issues.

9. Temporary Server Outages

Occasionally, Dropbox may experience server downtime, which can affect login functionality.

Solution:

1. Visit Dropbox's status page at status.dropbox.com to check for reported outages.
2. Wait for the issue to be resolved by Dropbox's technical team.
3. If the problem persists after the outage is resolved, contact Dropbox Support for further assistance.

By following these steps, you can resolve most login issues quickly and efficiently. If you encounter a persistent problem, remember that Dropbox Support and its robust Help Center are excellent resources for further assistance.

6.1.3 File Upload Errors

File upload errors are among the most common challenges faced by Dropbox users. These errors can arise from a variety of causes, including network issues, file limitations, or software glitches. In this section, we'll explore the common reasons for file upload failures and provide detailed solutions to ensure your files are uploaded successfully.

Understanding File Upload Errors

Before diving into specific solutions, it's essential to understand the potential causes of upload errors:

- **Network Connectivity Issues**: Slow or unstable internet connections are a primary culprit.

- **File Restrictions**: Files exceeding Dropbox's size limit or containing unsupported characters can cause errors.

- **Storage Limit Exceeded**: If your Dropbox account is at capacity, additional uploads may fail.

- **File Corruption**: A corrupted file may not upload properly.

- **Software Conflicts**: Outdated or incompatible Dropbox apps may interfere with uploads.

Step-by-Step Troubleshooting

1. Check Your Internet Connection

- **Verify Speed and Stability**: Use an online tool to check your internet speed. A minimum upload speed of 1 Mbps is recommended for smooth file transfers.

- **Switch Networks**: If you're on a public or unstable Wi-Fi network, try switching to a private or wired connection.

- **Restart Your Router**: Sometimes, simply restarting your modem or router can resolve network issues.

2. Review File Specifications

- **File Size**: Ensure your file is under Dropbox's upload limit for your plan (e.g., 2 GB for free accounts via the web interface).
- **File Type**: Verify that the file type is supported by Dropbox. Most file formats, including documents, images, and videos, are accepted.
- **File Name Restrictions**: Rename files that contain special characters such as "/," "?," or "*," as these are not allowed in Dropbox.

3. Monitor Available Storage

- **Check Account Storage**: Navigate to the account settings in the Dropbox web interface to see how much storage you've used.
- **Free Up Space**: Delete unnecessary files or move older files to an external drive. Consider upgrading your plan if you frequently encounter storage limitations.

4. Update Your Dropbox App

- **Check for Updates**: Ensure you're using the latest version of the Dropbox app. Updates often include fixes for known bugs and compatibility issues.
- **Reinstall the App**: Uninstall and reinstall the app to resolve potential corruption or misconfiguration.

5. Test the File on Another Device

- **Upload from Another Device**: If the issue persists on your current device, try uploading the file from a different one to rule out device-specific problems.
- **Use the Web Interface**: If the desktop or mobile app fails, try uploading your file directly via Dropbox's web interface.

6. Resolve Specific Error Messages

Dropbox often provides error codes or messages that offer clues to the problem. Here are some common ones:

- **"Upload Failed: Unknown Error"**: Restart the app or try uploading via the web interface.

- **"Storage Full"**: Delete files or upgrade your plan.
- **"File is Too Large"**: Compress the file or split it into smaller parts using a tool like WinRAR or 7-Zip.

Preventing Future Upload Errors

1. Optimize Your Workflow

- **Batch Uploads**: Instead of uploading many files at once, break them into smaller batches to avoid overwhelming your network or the app.
- **Scheduled Uploads**: Upload during off-peak hours to minimize the impact of slow networks.

2. Maintain Your Devices

- **Regular Updates**: Keep your operating system and Dropbox app updated to the latest versions.
- **Disk Cleanup**: Ensure your device has enough free storage to process uploads efficiently.

3. Use Dropbox Smart Sync

- Enable **Smart Sync** to keep local storage usage low while ensuring all files are accessible in the cloud. This feature prevents errors related to device storage limitations.

4. Monitor File Integrity

- **Verify Files Before Uploading**: Use file repair tools to check for corruption in large or critical files.
- **Scan for Malware**: Run antivirus software to ensure files are not infected with viruses, which may cause upload failures.

Advanced Troubleshooting Tips

1. Use Dropbox Debug Logs

Dropbox maintains logs that can help identify issues during file uploads:

- Access logs by clicking the Dropbox icon and navigating to **Help > View Logs**.
- Share these logs with Dropbox support for further analysis if needed.

2. Adjust Bandwidth Settings

- **Throttle Upload Speeds**: In Dropbox settings, limit upload speed to stabilize transfers over slow connections.
- **Disable Throttling**: Conversely, remove speed limits for faster uploads on strong connections.

3. Utilize Offline Uploads

For large files, consider using an offline upload feature:

- Save files locally and sync them to Dropbox when connected to a stable network.

When to Contact Support

If all else fails, it's time to seek help from Dropbox's support team. Provide the following information for a quicker resolution:

- File name and size.
- Error messages encountered.
- Steps you've already tried.
- Log files from the Dropbox app.

How to Contact Support:

- Use the in-app **Help Center** to initiate a support ticket.
- For faster assistance, consider upgrading to a Dropbox plan with priority support.

By following these troubleshooting steps, you'll not only resolve file upload errors but also improve your overall experience with Dropbox. Ensuring smooth and efficient file management will empower you to make the most of this powerful cloud storage solution.

6.2 Getting Help

6.2.1 Using the Help Center

Dropbox provides an extensive and user-friendly Help Center, designed to assist users in resolving issues, learning new features, and maximizing the platform's potential. Whether you're troubleshooting a specific problem, seeking best practices, or exploring advanced functionalities, the Help Center is your go-to resource. This section will guide you on how to make the most out of Dropbox's Help Center.

What is the Help Center?

The Dropbox Help Center is an online knowledge base filled with articles, tutorials, FAQs, and troubleshooting guides curated by Dropbox experts. It is available 24/7 and regularly updated to include the latest information about new features, fixes, and best practices. The Help Center is structured to provide quick and easy access to information for users of all experience levels, from beginners to advanced professionals.

Key Features of the Help Center:

- **Search Functionality:** Allows users to find specific articles by typing keywords or phrases.
- **Categories and Topics:** Organized into sections like file management, security, sharing, and billing.
- **Interactive Tutorials:** Step-by-step guides to help users learn how to perform tasks efficiently.
- **FAQs:** Answers to commonly asked questions from the Dropbox community.
- **Support Resources:** Links to additional support options, such as forums and direct contact methods.

How to Access the Help Center

Accessing the Help Center is simple and can be done from any device with an internet connection.

1. **Via the Dropbox Website:**

    o   Open your web browser and navigate to help.dropbox.com.

    o   Bookmark the page for easy access in the future.

2. **From the Dropbox Desktop App:**

    o   Click on your profile icon in the top-right corner of the Dropbox app.

    o   Select **Help Center** from the dropdown menu.

3. **Using the Mobile App:**

    o   Open the Dropbox mobile app.

    o   Tap the menu (usually three lines in the top-left corner).

    o   Scroll down and select **Help Center** under the Support section.

4. **From Search Engines:**

    o   Simply type your query into a search engine, followed by "Dropbox Help Center."

    o   Example: "How to restore deleted files Dropbox Help Center."

Finding Solutions Quickly

The Help Center is designed for efficiency, ensuring that users can quickly find the information they need. Here are tips to navigate it effectively:

Using the Search Bar

The search bar is the most powerful tool in the Help Center. Located prominently on the homepage, it allows users to type specific queries or keywords. For example:

- "How to share folders"
- "Fix Dropbox sync issues"

- "Upgrade Dropbox plan"

The search results are ranked by relevance, so the most helpful articles appear first. Use filters to refine your results, such as choosing articles updated within the last year or sorting by topic categories.

Exploring Categories

If you're unsure what to search for, browse through categories. The main categories include:

- **Account Management:** Covers account creation, settings, and billing.
- **File and Folder Management:** Guides on uploading, organizing, and sharing files.
- **Sync and Storage:** Solutions to syncing issues and storage limitations.
- **Security and Privacy:** Articles on two-factor authentication, permissions, and data safety.

Using the "Popular Articles" Section

The Help Center often highlights trending articles based on common user queries. These include guides on:

- Recovering deleted files.
- Setting up team accounts.
- Troubleshooting sync delays.

Reading Step-by-Step Tutorials

For visual learners, Dropbox provides detailed tutorials with screenshots or videos. These tutorials are particularly helpful for performing complex tasks, like integrating Dropbox with third-party tools or using Dropbox Paper effectively.

When to Use the Help Center

The Help Center is ideal for situations where you:

- Need immediate assistance and don't want to wait for support responses.

- Prefer self-learning over contacting customer service.
- Encounter common issues, such as syncing errors or login troubles.
- Want to explore new features or optimize your workflow with Dropbox.

Examples:

- **Scenario 1:** You accidentally deleted a file and want to recover it. The Help Center can guide you step-by-step.
- **Scenario 2:** Your account is running out of storage, and you're unsure how to upgrade. An article in the billing section provides instructions.
- **Scenario 3:** You want to learn how to share a folder with restricted access. Tutorials and FAQs will walk you through the process.

Advantages of the Help Center

- **Cost-Effective:** All resources are free to access, saving you the cost of professional support.
- **Time-Saving:** Immediate access to solutions without waiting for email responses or call-back times.
- **Expertly Curated:** Articles are created and reviewed by Dropbox professionals, ensuring accuracy.
- **Always Available:** Unlike customer support teams, the Help Center is accessible anytime, even during holidays or off-peak hours.

Additional Tips for Using the Help Center

1. **Bookmark Useful Articles:** Save frequently used guides for future reference.
2. **Check the Date of Articles:** Dropbox updates its platform regularly, so ensure you're reading the latest version.

3. **Use Multiple Queries:** If the first search doesn't yield results, try alternative keywords or phrases.

4. **Engage with Interactive Tools:** Some tutorials include downloadable templates or examples you can practice with.

When to Move Beyond the Help Center

While the Help Center is comprehensive, there are times when additional support may be necessary:

- If your issue involves account security or billing disputes, direct contact with Dropbox support is recommended.

- For technical errors not resolved by articles, the Dropbox support team or community forums may provide more personalized assistance.

In these cases, the Help Center will often redirect you to appropriate resources, such as email support or live chat options.

By mastering the Dropbox Help Center, you'll gain confidence in managing your account, troubleshooting issues, and discovering the full potential of Dropbox. Whether you're a beginner or an experienced user, the Help Center is an invaluable tool in your cloud storage journey.

6.2.2 Contacting Dropbox Support

When using Dropbox, encountering issues that require professional assistance is inevitable for many users, especially when dealing with complex problems. Dropbox Support offers a range of resources and services tailored to help users resolve their challenges efficiently. This section provides a comprehensive guide on how to contact Dropbox Support, the types of support available, and best practices for resolving issues effectively.

Understanding Dropbox Support Options

Dropbox offers different levels of support depending on your subscription plan. While free users have access to basic resources like help articles and community forums, premium users benefit from more personalized assistance, such as direct email or live chat support. Understanding these options can help you determine the best way to get the assistance you need.

1. **Basic (Free) Plan Support:**

    o Access to an extensive online **Help Center** filled with articles and tutorials.

    o Participation in the **Community Forums**, where users and moderators share solutions.

2. **Plus and Family Plan Support:**

    o Email support with priority response times.

    o Access to live chat during business hours for faster issue resolution.

3. **Professional and Business Plans:**

    o Priority email and live chat support.

    o **Phone support** for business plans, ideal for urgent matters.

    o Dedicated **account managers** for large teams.

When to Contact Dropbox Support

Before contacting Dropbox Support, it's important to evaluate the complexity of your issue. Many minor problems can be resolved through self-service tools like the Help Center or community forums. Consider contacting support if:

- You encounter **technical errors** such as sync issues or file recovery problems.
- Your account is **compromised** or you suspect unauthorized access.

CHAPTER VI: TROUBLESHOOTING AND FAQS

- You have **billing inquiries** or need assistance with subscription changes.
- You require help with **advanced integrations** or team account configurations.

How to Reach Dropbox Support

Dropbox provides multiple channels for contacting their support team. Below is a step-by-step guide for accessing each method:

1. **Email Support:**
    - Log in to your Dropbox account and navigate to the **Help Center**.
    - Click on **Contact Us** at the bottom of the page.
    - Select the **Email Support** option and fill out the form with details about your issue.
    - Include screenshots or relevant files to help the support team diagnose the problem.
    - Once submitted, you'll receive a confirmation email with a reference number. Dropbox typically responds within 24–48 hours for premium users and slightly longer for free accounts.

2. **Live Chat Support:**
    - Available for paid users, this feature can be accessed through the **Help Center**.
    - Click on **Contact Us**, select your topic, and choose **Chat with Us**.
    - A chat window will open, connecting you to a support agent in real-time.
    - Use live chat for time-sensitive issues like troubleshooting syncing problems or recovering recently deleted files.

3. **Phone Support (Business Accounts Only):**
    - If you are a business account user, you can find the phone support number in your **Admin Console**.

- Prepare relevant information, such as your account details and a description of the problem, before calling.
- Note that phone support is often available during business hours and may vary by region.

4. **Support Ticket System:**
    - For complex issues, Dropbox allows you to create a detailed support ticket.
    - Include as much information as possible, such as error messages, timestamps, and affected files.

Tips for Contacting Dropbox Support

To ensure a smooth experience when reaching out to Dropbox Support, consider the following best practices:

1. **Be Specific and Clear:**
    - Clearly explain your issue, providing relevant details such as the device you're using, your operating system, and any error messages you've encountered.

2. **Attach Screenshots or Videos:**
    - Visual aids can help the support team better understand your problem and expedite the resolution process.

3. **Check Your Email Regularly:**
    - Stay updated on responses from Dropbox Support. Reply promptly if they request additional information.

4. **Be Patient and Courteous:**
    - Keep in mind that support teams handle numerous queries daily. Being polite and patient can make your interaction more pleasant and productive.

Common Scenarios and Solutions with Dropbox Support

1. **Recovering Deleted Files:**
   - If you accidentally delete a file and can't recover it from the Deleted Files section, Dropbox Support can assist in retrieving it, provided it falls within the recovery window for your plan.

2. **Syncing Issues:**
   - When troubleshooting syncing problems, Dropbox Support might guide you through clearing cache files, resetting the app, or updating your software.

3. **Account Access Issues:**
   - In cases where you are locked out of your account due to password problems or two-factor authentication issues, support can verify your identity and help restore access.

4. **Billing and Subscription Questions:**
   - For billing disputes or subscription downgrades, Dropbox Support can provide detailed explanations and process any required changes.

Benefits of Contacting Dropbox Support

1. **Expert Assistance:**
   - Support representatives are trained to handle complex technical issues efficiently.

2. **Time Savings:**
   - Instead of troubleshooting on your own, professional guidance can lead to quicker resolutions.

3. **Peace of Mind:**

o   Knowing that experts are handling your issue allows you to focus on your work or other priorities.

Dropbox Support is an invaluable resource for users at all levels. By understanding the available options and following best practices, you can resolve issues effectively and make the most of your Dropbox experience. Whether you're dealing with minor technical hiccups or urgent account problems, the support team is there to help every step of the way.

6.2.3 Community Forums and Tips

When navigating the world of Dropbox, community forums and expert tips can serve as invaluable resources. They provide not only solutions to specific problems but also insights into how others are maximizing their Dropbox experience. This section explores the role of community forums, offers guidance on using them effectively, and shares tips that can save time, improve productivity, and deepen your understanding of Dropbox.

Understanding the Role of Community Forums

Community forums are online spaces where Dropbox users—from beginners to experts—gather to share knowledge, troubleshoot issues, and exchange advice. These forums are typically hosted by Dropbox itself or established on third-party platforms by dedicated enthusiasts. They can be especially helpful for:

1. **Troubleshooting Complex Issues:** Many problems have already been experienced and resolved by other users. Searching the forum can often provide instant solutions.

2. **Learning Advanced Techniques:** Users frequently share tips for power features, like workflow automation or file organization strategies, which may not be well-documented elsewhere.

3. **Staying Informed:** Forums are great places to discover user feedback on new features, beta updates, or even upcoming changes to Dropbox services.

How to Use Community Forums Effectively

1. Finding the Right Forum

To begin, ensure you are accessing a reputable and active community. Here are some of the best places to start:

- **Dropbox Community Forum:** Hosted by Dropbox, this is the official space where users and staff interact. Visit at community.dropbox.com.

- **Reddit Communities:** Subreddits like r/Dropbox often feature discussions, user tips, and solutions from tech-savvy individuals.

- **Technology Forums:** Broader forums like Stack Overflow or Quora can also be helpful for specific Dropbox-related questions.

2. Searching for Solutions

Forums often have powerful search tools. Here's how to make the most of them:

- **Use Keywords:** Be specific. Instead of "file issue," try "Dropbox file won't upload error code 404."

- **Browse by Categories:** Many forums organize discussions into topics such as troubleshooting, account management, or integrations.

- **Check Resolved Threads:** Look for posts marked as resolved, as these often provide concise and effective answers.

3. Engaging with the Community

Don't just passively consume content—engage with the community for a richer experience:

- **Ask Clear Questions:** When posting a query, include details such as the device, operating system, and a description of the issue.

- **Provide Feedback:** If you find a solution, reply with a "thank you" or additional insights to help others.

- **Participate in Discussions:** Sharing your experiences can be just as valuable as receiving advice.

Essential Tips from Dropbox Users

1. Mastering Sync Features

One common challenge users face is ensuring their files sync correctly across devices. Forum users recommend:

- **Checking Bandwidth Settings:** Adjust your Dropbox preferences to allocate more bandwidth if syncing is slow.
- **Using Selective Sync:** This feature lets you choose which folders to sync locally, saving space and speeding up processes.

2. Maximizing Productivity

Experienced Dropbox users often share productivity hacks, such as:

- **Utilizing Keyboard Shortcuts:** Forums frequently compile lists of shortcuts for quick navigation and file management.
- **Automating Workflows with Third-Party Tools:** Many community members highlight apps like Zapier or IFTTT for automating repetitive Dropbox tasks.

3. Enhancing Security

Security is a recurring topic in forums. Tips include:

- **Frequent Password Updates:** Change your password periodically and avoid reusing it across other platforms.
- **Using Two-Factor Authentication (2FA):** Enable this for an added layer of protection, as recommended by both users and experts.

Common Challenges and Community Solutions

Forums are a treasure trove of practical solutions. Here are a few commonly discussed challenges and the advice often shared:

Problem: Files Aren't Syncing Properly

- **Solution:** Ensure you have sufficient local storage and check your internet connection. If syncing is still slow, unlink and relink your account to refresh the connection.

Problem: Can't Access Shared Files

- **Solution:** Verify the permissions set by the file owner. Many users suggest contacting the owner to ensure you have view or edit rights.

Problem: Large Files Won't Upload

- **Solution:** Break the file into smaller parts using file compression tools, then upload them individually or use the "Upload via Link" feature.

Building Your Knowledge Through Forums

Forums are not only for troubleshooting—they're educational resources too. Here's how to deepen your Dropbox expertise:

1. Learn About Beta Features

Many forums include dedicated threads for beta testers. Participating in these discussions can provide early access to new Dropbox features and insights into how they work.

2. Explore Use Cases

Users frequently share how they leverage Dropbox in real-world scenarios, such as managing business projects, organizing family photos, or collaborating on creative works.

3. Develop Technical Skills

Active participation in forums can expose you to technical topics like APIs, integration with tools like Zapier, and advanced features like Smart Sync.

Final Thoughts on Community Forums and Tips

Community forums are a dynamic and supportive environment for Dropbox users. Whether you're seeking help for a pressing issue or looking to become a Dropbox power user, these platforms are rich in resources. The more you contribute, the more value you'll derive—not only in solving problems but also in expanding your knowledge and fostering connections with fellow users.

6.3 Staying Updated

6.3.1 New Features and Announcements

Staying informed about new features and updates in Dropbox is crucial for maximizing your experience with the platform. Dropbox is a dynamic service, constantly evolving to meet the needs of individuals, teams, and businesses. This section will guide you on how to stay updated with Dropbox's latest developments and explain why keeping up with these changes is beneficial.

Why Staying Updated Matters

Technology moves quickly, and cloud storage solutions are no exception. By staying informed about Dropbox's updates, you can:

1. **Enhance Productivity**: New features often introduce tools to simplify workflows and improve efficiency.

2. **Improve Security**: Updates frequently address security vulnerabilities and introduce enhanced measures to protect your data.

3. **Leverage Integrations**: Dropbox regularly improves compatibility with third-party tools, offering better collaboration options.

4. **Access New Functionalities**: Staying current allows you to take full advantage of innovative features that save time and effort.

How Dropbox Communicates Updates

Dropbox uses multiple channels to announce new features and improvements. Understanding where to find this information ensures you're always in the loop:

1. **Product Blog**

Dropbox's official product blog is a primary source for announcements. Here, the company shares detailed posts about new tools, design changes, and integrations.

- o Visit the blog regularly to read about upcoming rollouts and their potential benefits.
- o Subscribe to the newsletter to receive updates directly in your email inbox.

2. **In-App Notifications**

The Dropbox app provides timely notifications about updates. These appear as banners or pop-ups on both desktop and mobile platforms.

- o Check for announcements in the dashboard or the help section.
- o Pay attention to prompts suggesting new ways to use Dropbox.

3. **Social Media Channels**

Dropbox is active on platforms like Twitter, LinkedIn, and Facebook, where it shares concise updates, user stories, and feature highlights.

- o Follow Dropbox on your preferred social media platform to get quick updates.
- o Engage with posts to learn from other users' experiences and tips.

4. **Release Notes**

Detailed release notes are available on the Dropbox website and app stores.

- o These notes include technical specifics about updates and fixes.
- o Review them after installing app updates to learn what's new.

5. **Webinars and Live Events**

Dropbox occasionally hosts webinars to showcase major feature releases.

- o Attend these events to see demonstrations and ask questions directly to Dropbox experts.

Understanding Major Updates

Dropbox's updates typically fall into several categories:

1. **User Interface (UI) Enhancements**

    Dropbox often refines its interface to make navigation more intuitive. For instance, they may add streamlined menus or reorganize tool placement to improve usability.

    - Recent examples include a redesigned mobile app layout and a revamped file preview experience.
    - Familiarize yourself with changes by exploring the updated interface and reading any accompanying guides.

2. **Collaboration Tools**

    Enhancements in collaboration tools aim to facilitate teamwork. New features may include improved shared folder management, real-time notifications, or better integrations with platforms like Slack and Microsoft Teams.

    - For example, Dropbox Spaces, an advanced collaboration tool, was introduced to allow teams to work on shared projects seamlessly.
    - Keep track of such updates to optimize team workflows.

3. **Performance Improvements**

    Many updates focus on behind-the-scenes changes that improve app speed, reduce sync times, or enhance reliability.

    - Regularly update your Dropbox app to ensure you benefit from these optimizations.

4. **New Integrations and Features**

    Dropbox frequently expands its integration capabilities, allowing users to connect with popular tools such as Zoom, Canva, and Trello.

    - Explore these integrations to add functionality tailored to your needs.

5. **Security Enhancements**

Security is a top priority for Dropbox. Updates may include new encryption protocols, two-factor authentication improvements, or better user access controls.

- Review security-related updates promptly to implement recommended measures.

Making the Most of New Features

After learning about new features, it's essential to put them into practice. Here's how you can adapt effectively:

1. **Experiment with Features**

    Try out newly introduced tools or settings. For example, if Dropbox introduces an improved sharing interface, test it by sharing files with colleagues or friends.

2. **Review Tutorials**

    Dropbox often provides video tutorials or step-by-step guides to help users get acquainted with new features. These resources can be found on their blog or YouTube channel.

3. **Provide Feedback**

    Engage with Dropbox by sharing your feedback on new updates. Use in-app surveys or participate in beta testing programs to contribute to the platform's development.

4. **Incorporate Features into Workflows**

    Identify how new functionalities can simplify your daily tasks. For example, if Dropbox launches a feature for document signing, consider using it for contracts or official forms.

Staying Proactive

To stay ahead, adopt proactive habits:

1. **Enable Auto-Updates**

   Keep your Dropbox app set to update automatically. This ensures you receive the latest features as soon as they're released.

2. **Join User Communities**

   Participate in forums and online groups where users discuss Dropbox updates. These communities can provide insights into best practices and potential use cases.

3. **Monitor Competitors**

   Sometimes, updates are inspired by advancements in competing platforms. Understanding these trends helps you anticipate Dropbox's future improvements.

Examples of Recent Features

Here are a few notable features Dropbox has introduced recently to illustrate the importance of staying updated:

1. **Dropbox Passwords**: A tool for managing and securing passwords across devices.
2. **Dropbox Vault**: An extra layer of protection for sensitive files.
3. **Automatic Backup**: A feature that allows users to back up their entire computer effortlessly.
4. **Dropbox Replay**: A review and feedback tool for video creators.

By understanding and utilizing these tools, users can enhance their overall Dropbox experience.

Conclusion

Staying informed about Dropbox's new features and updates is key to maximizing your productivity, security, and overall experience. By leveraging multiple channels to receive updates, actively experimenting with new tools, and integrating them into your workflows, you ensure that your Dropbox usage remains effective and relevant. As Dropbox continues to evolve, staying updated guarantees you'll always be ahead of the curve in cloud storage management.

6.3.2 Beta Testing Dropbox Features

Beta testing is an essential process for companies like Dropbox to refine their features before releasing them to the general public. By participating in Dropbox's beta testing programs, you not only get early access to new and innovative tools but also contribute to the platform's improvement by providing feedback. This section will explore the benefits of beta testing, how to join Dropbox's beta testing program, and best practices for providing useful feedback.

What is Beta Testing?

Beta testing involves trying out pre-release versions of features or updates to evaluate their functionality and performance. These beta versions may have bugs or incomplete elements, as their purpose is to test real-world use cases and gather insights from users. By joining a beta program, you become a part of the product development process, helping Dropbox create a better and more reliable experience for its users.

Benefits of Beta Testing Dropbox Features

1. **Early Access to New Tools:**

   As a beta tester, you can explore Dropbox's latest features before they are officially rolled out. This advantage allows you to stay ahead of the curve, gaining insight into new functionality and seeing how it might enhance your workflow.

2. **Influencing Product Development:**

   Your feedback during beta testing plays a crucial role in shaping the final product. Dropbox values input from its users, and beta testers often have a significant impact on design tweaks, feature enhancements, or even the decision to move forward with a particular tool.

3. **Improved Technical Expertise:**

   By engaging with experimental features, you develop a deeper understanding of Dropbox's capabilities. This hands-on experience can be particularly useful for tech-savvy professionals looking to maximize their use of cloud storage solutions.

4. **Community** **Involvement:**
   Joining the beta testing community allows you to interact with like-minded users who share their insights and experiences. This networking opportunity fosters collaboration and provides additional learning opportunities.

How to Join Dropbox's Beta Testing Program

Becoming a Dropbox beta tester is a straightforward process. Here's a step-by-step guide to get started:

1. **Sign Up for the Beta Program:**

   - Visit Dropbox's official beta program webpage. Look for links or announcements on the Dropbox forums or help center that invite users to join.

   - Complete the application process by logging into your Dropbox account and expressing your interest in participating.

2. **Enable Beta Features in Your Account Settings:**

   - Log into your Dropbox account on the web.

   - Navigate to the **Settings** page, and look for the **Beta Features** section.

   - Toggle the switch to enable beta features. You may also need to agree to terms regarding the use of experimental tools.

3. **Download the Beta Version of Dropbox Apps:**

   - If the beta program involves testing updates to the Dropbox desktop or mobile apps, you'll need to download and install the beta version of the application.

- Follow the provided instructions carefully to avoid overwriting your stable version if you wish to keep both.

4. **Stay Informed:**
    - Beta programs often come with updates or instructions on what features to test. Keep an eye on your email, the Dropbox forums, or the beta testing portal for specific guidelines.

Best Practices for Beta Testing

1. **Explore Features Thoroughly:**

    Take time to use the new features in various scenarios to understand their strengths and limitations. For instance, if you are testing a new file-sharing tool, try it with different file types and sizes to see how it performs.

2. **Document Issues:**
    - Keep a record of any issues or bugs you encounter, including steps to reproduce them.
    - Note details like your operating system, app version, and any relevant error messages.

3. **Provide Constructive Feedback:**
    - Share your thoughts on what works well and what could be improved.
    - Be specific and objective. For example, instead of saying "This doesn't work," explain, "The feature failed when I attempted to upload a 2GB file on macOS."

4. **Engage with the Community:**

    Join discussions with other beta testers in the Dropbox forums. Sharing your experiences can help others troubleshoot issues and provide additional insights for Dropbox's development team.

5. **Follow Beta Program Guidelines:**

Adhere to the instructions and focus areas provided by Dropbox. Avoid relying on beta features for critical tasks, as they may not function perfectly.

Understanding the Risks of Beta Testing

While beta testing has many benefits, there are some risks and challenges to consider:

1. **Stability Issues:**

    Beta features might be unstable and prone to crashes. Ensure you have backups of important files before using beta software.

2. **Incomplete Features:**

    Some tools may be in early stages of development, meaning they might lack full functionality or polished interfaces.

3. **Confidentiality Requirements:**

    In some cases, Dropbox might require you to sign a non-disclosure agreement (NDA) to prevent sharing information about unreleased features.

Dropbox's Commitment to Beta Testers

Dropbox strives to make beta testing a positive and rewarding experience for its participants. The company provides several resources to support testers:

1. **Detailed Release Notes:**

    Beta testers receive comprehensive updates about what's new in each release, ensuring clarity on what to test.

2. **Support Channels:**

    Dropbox offers dedicated support options for beta participants, including forums and feedback submission forms.

3. **User Acknowledgment:**

Dropbox often recognizes outstanding beta testers by incorporating their feedback or publicly thanking them in updates.

Making the Most of Beta Testing

To maximize your experience as a beta tester, consider these tips:

- Use beta features alongside your regular workflows to test real-life scenarios.
- Regularly check for updates to ensure you're testing the latest version.
- Maintain a separate folder or account for testing, so experimental features don't interfere with your primary files.

Conclusion

Beta testing Dropbox features is a unique opportunity to explore cutting-edge tools, shape the future of cloud storage, and contribute to the platform's growth. By following best practices and engaging with the community, you can make meaningful contributions while gaining early access to features that enhance your Dropbox experience.

6.3.3 Keeping Your Apps Up-to-Date

Staying updated with the latest version of the Dropbox application is essential for optimal performance, enhanced features, and improved security. Regular updates not only bring new functionalities but also ensure that your app is protected from vulnerabilities and remains compatible with other tools and systems you might use. This section will guide you through the importance of updates, how to manage them, and best practices to maintain an up-to-date Dropbox experience.

The Importance of Updates

Updates are the backbone of any modern software, and Dropbox is no exception. Here's why keeping your Dropbox app updated is crucial:

1. **Security Enhancements**: Cyber threats evolve constantly, and developers work tirelessly to patch vulnerabilities. Updates ensure your files and data remain safe from new risks.

2. **Improved Performance**: Updates often include performance optimizations, fixing bugs or glitches that could slow down the app or cause crashes.

3. **Access to New Features**: Dropbox regularly introduces new tools and functionalities to improve user experience. Without updates, you may miss out on these enhancements.

4. **Compatibility**: Operating systems and third-party tools frequently update. Keeping your Dropbox app updated ensures compatibility with these changes.

How to Check for Updates

On Desktop Applications

1. **Automatic Updates**: Dropbox is designed to update automatically on desktop systems. Ensure this feature is enabled in your settings to receive updates without manual intervention.

2. **Manual Update Check**:

    - On Windows:
        - Open Dropbox from the taskbar.
        - Go to **Preferences > General Tab**.
        - Check if there's a notification for an update. If available, follow the prompt to install.

    - On macOS:
        - Click on the Dropbox icon in the menu bar.

- Navigate to **Preferences > Account Tab** and look for update notifications.

On Mobile Applications

1. **iOS Devices**:

   o Open the **App Store**.

   o Tap your profile icon in the top-right corner.

   o Scroll to the list of apps and find Dropbox. If an update is available, tap "Update."

2. **Android Devices**:

   o Open the **Google Play Store**.

   o Tap the menu icon and go to **My Apps & Games**.

   o Look for Dropbox under the "Updates" section and tap "Update."

Setting Up Automatic Updates

Desktop Systems

Most operating systems support automatic updates for applications installed via their app stores. To enable this:

- **Windows**: Go to the Microsoft Store settings and enable automatic updates.

- **macOS**: Open the App Store, go to preferences, and enable **Automatic Updates** for installed apps.

Mobile Devices

1. **iOS**:

   o Go to **Settings > App Store**.

   o Toggle on **App Updates** to enable automatic updates for all apps, including Dropbox.

2. **Android**:

    o Open the Google Play Store.

    o Go to **Settings > Auto-Update Apps** and select **Over Wi-Fi Only** to save mobile data.

Dealing with Update Issues

Sometimes, updates might fail or encounter issues. Here's how to handle such problems:

1. **Insufficient Storage**:

    Ensure your device has enough free space to download and install updates. On mobile devices, consider clearing app caches or deleting unnecessary files to free up space.

2. **Slow Internet Connection**:

    A stable and fast connection is essential for downloading updates. If your update is taking too long, switch to a stronger Wi-Fi network or check your internet speed.

3. **Incompatibility**:

    o Check if your operating system meets the minimum requirements for the latest version of Dropbox.

    o If your OS is outdated, consider updating it or using the web version of Dropbox until you can upgrade your system.

4. **Manual Reinstallation**:

    o If an update fails repeatedly, uninstall the app and reinstall the latest version from the official website or app store.

Tips for Staying Updated

1. **Enable Notifications**: Allow Dropbox to send you notifications about new updates. This ensures you're aware of improvements or necessary actions.

2. **Check Update Logs**: Visit the official Dropbox release notes page to understand what changes or enhancements are included in the latest updates.

3. **Schedule Regular Checks**: If you prefer manual updates, set a monthly reminder to check for updates across your devices.

4. **Join Beta Programs**: For tech-savvy users, joining Dropbox's beta program can give you early access to new features while helping the team refine the software.

Benefits of Regular Updates

By maintaining the latest version of Dropbox, users often notice:

- **Better Sync Speeds**: Updated versions optimize sync algorithms for faster uploads and downloads.

- **Enhanced Collaboration Tools**: Updates might improve features like commenting or real-time edits.

- **New Integrations**: Dropbox often integrates with popular third-party tools to enhance productivity.

- **Smoother User Experience**: Frequent updates polish the interface, making it more intuitive and user-friendly.

Conclusion

Keeping your Dropbox app up-to-date is a simple yet powerful way to maximize its potential. Whether it's gaining access to new features, ensuring top-notch security, or maintaining seamless compatibility, regular updates should be part of your digital routine. By following the strategies outlined in this section, you'll ensure your Dropbox experience remains efficient, secure, and enjoyable.

CHAPTER VI: TROUBLESHOOTING AND FAQS

Conclusion

7.1 Recap of Key Features

Dropbox has become one of the most popular and trusted cloud storage platforms available, thanks to its rich array of features and seamless user experience. This section revisits the essential features that make Dropbox an indispensable tool for individuals and businesses alike. Understanding these features not only reinforces your grasp of Dropbox's capabilities but also helps you maximize its potential.

File Storage and Accessibility

At its core, Dropbox offers reliable cloud storage for all your digital files. Whether it's documents, photos, videos, or presentations, Dropbox provides a secure space for your data. The platform excels in:

- **Cross-Device Accessibility:** Your files are accessible on any device with an internet connection, including desktops, tablets, and smartphones. This ensures that your important files are always within reach, whether at work, home, or on the go.

- **Offline Access:** You can mark specific files and folders for offline access, allowing you to work without an internet connection. Any changes made offline are automatically synced when you reconnect.

- **Scalable Storage Plans:** Dropbox offers plans ranging from free accounts with 2 GB of storage to professional and business plans with terabytes of space, catering to various user needs.

File Sharing and Collaboration

Dropbox is more than just a storage platform—it's a powerful tool for sharing and collaboration. Its sharing features are intuitive and customizable, making it easy to collaborate on projects of any size.

- **Simple Sharing Links:** Dropbox allows you to generate shareable links for any file or folder. These links can be shared via email, chat, or even embedded in websites.

- **Custom Permissions:** You control how others interact with your files. Options include view-only access, editing permissions, or restricting downloads altogether.

- **Shared Folders:** Collaborators can work together in shared folders, with all changes syncing in real time. This is particularly useful for teams working on shared projects.

- **Dropbox Paper Integration:** Dropbox Paper, a collaborative workspace, enables real-time editing, brainstorming, and project management within the Dropbox ecosystem.

Syncing and Version Control

Dropbox's syncing capabilities are seamless and efficient, ensuring your files are up-to-date across all devices.

- **Automatic Syncing:** Files uploaded or modified on one device are instantly synced across all linked devices, minimizing the risk of outdated versions.

- **Selective Sync:** You can choose which folders to sync locally, saving space on your hard drive.

- **Version History:** Dropbox retains a history of changes for up to 180 days (depending on your plan), allowing you to restore previous versions of files or recover deleted ones. This feature is invaluable for mitigating accidental deletions or overwriting important data.

Advanced Security and Privacy

Security is a top priority for Dropbox, making it a trustworthy platform for personal and professional use.

- **Data Encryption:** Dropbox employs industry-standard encryption for both data at rest and in transit.

- **Two-Factor Authentication (2FA):** Adding an extra layer of security, 2FA ensures only authorized users can access your account.

- **Granular Access Controls:** You can manage permissions at the file or folder level, allowing or restricting access as needed.

- **Compliance:** Dropbox adheres to various industry standards and regulations, including GDPR and HIPAA (for business accounts), making it suitable for handling sensitive data.

Integrations with Other Tools

One of Dropbox's most powerful features is its ability to integrate seamlessly with third-party applications and platforms.

- **Microsoft Office and Google Workspace:** Edit Word, Excel, and Google Docs directly from Dropbox without downloading the files.

- **Slack, Trello, and Zoom:** Collaborate efficiently by linking Dropbox to team communication and project management tools.

- **APIs for Developers:** For businesses with custom software needs, Dropbox's API enables tailored integrations.

Productivity Features

Dropbox goes beyond storage with features designed to boost productivity.

- **Smart Sync:** Automatically manage your storage by keeping infrequently used files in the cloud while making them appear locally on your device.

- **File Requests:** Collect files from clients or collaborators easily, even if they don't have a Dropbox account.

- **Document Scanning:** Using the mobile app, you can scan and upload physical documents directly to Dropbox.

- **Dropbox Transfer:** Send large files securely with a dedicated transfer tool, which includes tracking and customizable branding options for business users.

Mobile App Features

Dropbox's mobile app brings powerful functionality to your smartphone or tablet.

- **Camera Uploads:** Automatically back up photos and videos from your device.
- **On-the-Go File Editing:** Edit and comment on files directly in the app.
- **Mobile Notifications:** Stay updated on file activity and shared folder changes in real time.
- **Voice Commands:** For supported devices, use voice commands to search for files or perform specific actions.

Team Management and Collaboration for Businesses

For organizations, Dropbox offers tailored features to enhance teamwork and file management.

- **Admin Controls:** Manage user access, monitor activity, and enforce policies across the organization.
- **Team Spaces:** Create centralized hubs where teams can share and organize files collectively.
- **Audit Logs:** Track user actions for compliance and security purposes.
- **Priority Support:** Business accounts come with dedicated support to resolve issues quickly.

The Future of Dropbox

Dropbox continues to evolve, introducing new features and expanding its capabilities. Users can expect ongoing updates, such as:

- **AI and Machine Learning:** Enhanced file search and recommendations.
- **Deeper Integrations:** Broader compatibility with emerging tools and platforms.
- **Eco-Friendly Initiatives:** Dropbox's commitment to sustainability with energy-efficient data centers.

Conclusion

These features demonstrate why Dropbox remains a leader in the cloud storage industry. From file storage to team collaboration, Dropbox is a versatile platform that caters to both personal and professional needs. By mastering its features, you unlock the full potential of cloud storage, making your work more efficient, secure, and streamlined.

7.2 Tips for Maximizing Dropbox

Dropbox is a powerful tool that helps you store, organize, share, and collaborate on your files. While getting started with Dropbox is relatively simple, there are many advanced features and strategies that can help you make the most of this cloud storage platform. In this section, we'll cover tips and techniques for maximizing Dropbox's potential, ensuring that you're using it to its fullest capability.

1. Organize Your Files Efficiently

One of the most common challenges people face with cloud storage is keeping files organized. With Dropbox, it's easy to create a chaotic mess of files and folders, especially when dealing with large volumes of documents. A well-structured system for organizing your files will help you find them quickly, avoid duplicates, and stay efficient in your workflow.

- **Create a Folder Hierarchy**

    One of the best ways to stay organized in Dropbox is to create a logical folder structure. You can organize your files by project, department, or client, depending on the nature of your work. Use subfolders to further break down information into specific categories or dates. For instance, if you're managing a marketing campaign, you could create a folder titled "Marketing Campaigns," and within that, you can have subfolders like "Campaign A," "Campaign B," etc. This hierarchy will help you locate files faster and reduce clutter in your main folder.

- **Use Descriptive Folder and File Names**

    Always use clear, descriptive names for both folders and files. Avoid generic names like "Document1" or "Untitled Folder." Instead, name your files something that makes sense, such as "Quarterly_Report_2024" or "Client_Proposal_Draft." This will make searching for documents much more straightforward.

- **Leverage Dropbox's Search Function**

    Dropbox has a powerful search feature that allows you to find specific files in seconds. If your folder structure is well-organized and your file names are descriptive, you can use the search bar to locate exactly what you need without wasting time scrolling through countless folders. Make sure to use keywords that are relevant to the document or project you're working on. You can also filter your search by file type, date modified, or file owner, which further narrows down your results.

2. Sync Files Across All Devices

Dropbox's syncing feature is one of its key strengths. Whether you're working on your laptop, phone, or tablet, Dropbox ensures that your files are always up to date and accessible from any device. To maximize the syncing function, it's important to understand how Dropbox manages file synchronization.

- **Enable Selective Sync**

    Dropbox offers a feature called Selective Sync, which allows you to choose which folders to sync with your computer. This is particularly useful if you have limited storage space on your device but want to keep all your files in Dropbox. Simply right-click on a folder in Dropbox and select "Selective Sync." You can then select which folders you'd like to sync to your computer and which ones you'll only access through the web interface. By keeping only the essential folders synced, you can save storage space while still having access to everything you need.

- **Utilize Smart Sync for More Efficient Storage**

    If you're a Dropbox Plus, Family, Professional, or Business user, you can use the Smart Sync feature. This allows you to keep all your files in the cloud while appearing as though they are on your computer. With Smart Sync, you don't need to worry about storage space on your hard drive, as files that you're not actively working on will remain in the cloud, but you'll still be able to access them instantly when needed. This is an excellent way to maximize your storage without sacrificing accessibility.

- **Monitor Syncing Progress**

    Occasionally, syncing issues can arise, such as files not uploading correctly or syncing at a slow rate. To ensure that everything is synced properly, always check the sync status in the Dropbox app. A green checkmark means the file is synced, while a blue circular arrow indicates that syncing is in progress. If you see an error icon, Dropbox will provide details on what needs to be fixed.

3. Use Version History to Avoid Mistakes

Dropbox's version history feature allows you to view and restore previous versions of a file. This is invaluable if you've accidentally deleted content, made an unwanted change, or simply want to revert to an earlier version of a document. Many Dropbox users don't take full advantage of this feature, but it's an essential tool for anyone who handles important or sensitive files.

- **Accessing Version History**

    To view the version history of a file, right-click on the file in your Dropbox account and select "Version history." You'll be shown a list of previous versions of the file, and you can choose to restore any of these versions if necessary. This feature works for any file type, including Word documents, Excel spreadsheets, PDFs, images, and more.

- **Set File Retention Policies for Teams**

    If you're using Dropbox for Business, you can set retention policies for your files. This ensures that certain files are kept for a specified period of time and then automatically deleted after the retention period expires. It's particularly useful for compliance purposes or for reducing unnecessary clutter in your business's file storage.

4. Take Advantage of Collaboration Tools

Dropbox is not just a file storage platform; it also offers powerful collaboration features that make it easy for teams to work together, whether they're in the same office or located remotely. To truly maximize Dropbox, consider using the collaboration tools at your disposal.

- **Dropbox Paper for Real-Time Collaboration**

    Dropbox Paper is an online document editor that allows multiple users to collaborate in real time. You can write, edit, and comment on documents together, making it perfect for brainstorming sessions, project plans, or meeting notes. Dropbox Paper integrates seamlessly with other Dropbox files, and any changes made are automatically saved and synced across all devices.

- **Shared Folders for Group Projects**

If you're working with a team, consider using shared folders. A shared folder allows everyone with access to the folder to add, edit, and view files. This eliminates the need for back-and-forth email exchanges or file versioning confusion. You can also set permissions on shared folders, so you can control whether team members have edit, view, or comment access.

- **Use Comments and @mentions for Communication**

    Dropbox allows you to leave comments directly on files. This can be especially useful for providing feedback on documents or collaborating on ideas. You can also tag team members using the "@mention" feature, which sends them a notification so they can respond quickly. By keeping all communication in Dropbox, you can eliminate the need for external email threads and keep everything in one place.

5. Secure Your Files with Two-Factor Authentication

Dropbox offers several ways to secure your files, and one of the best ways to add an extra layer of protection is by enabling two-factor authentication (2FA). 2FA is a security feature that requires you to provide two forms of identification before accessing your account: your password and a code sent to your phone. This prevents unauthorized access, even if someone has your password.

- **Setting Up Two-Factor Authentication**

    To enable 2FA, log in to your Dropbox account, go to the Security section in your account settings, and follow the instructions to set up 2FA. You can choose to receive the code via text message or an authentication app like Google Authenticator. Once enabled, you'll be required to enter the code every time you log in from an unrecognized device.

- **Regularly Update Your Password**

    In addition to enabling 2FA, make sure to change your Dropbox password regularly. Use a strong, unique password that combines upper and lowercase letters, numbers, and special characters. Avoid reusing passwords from other accounts to minimize the risk of a security breach.

6. Use Dropbox for Business

If you run a business, Dropbox offers a suite of tools designed to help teams collaborate and manage their workflow more effectively. Dropbox Business provides enhanced storage options, advanced security features, and administrative tools to manage team members and files. Upgrading to Dropbox Business can help streamline operations and improve team productivity.

- **Admin Tools for Team Management**

    Dropbox Business allows admins to set up and manage teams, assign roles, and monitor team activity. You can see who is accessing your files, what they are working on, and how much storage space is being used. Admins can also set file-sharing policies and access controls to ensure that sensitive information remains secure.

- **Enhanced Storage and File Recovery**

    Dropbox Business offers unlimited storage and extended version history, allowing you to keep track of files and restore previous versions for up to 180 days. This feature is especially useful for businesses with a high volume of files or those that need to comply with data retention policies.

Conclusion

Maximizing Dropbox's potential requires more than just uploading files. By organizing your files efficiently, using collaboration tools, securing your account, and taking advantage of advanced features, you can turn Dropbox into a powerful tool that enhances your productivity and protects your data. Whether you're an individual user or part of a team, these tips will help you get the most out of Dropbox, ensuring that your files are organized, secure, and accessible whenever you need them.

7.3 Final Thoughts on Cloud Storage

In the digital age, cloud storage has become an integral part of both personal and professional life. Whether you're storing personal documents, collaborating with colleagues, or managing vast amounts of data, cloud storage systems like Dropbox offer unmatched convenience, security, and accessibility. As we've explored in this book, Dropbox is more than just a storage solution; it is a comprehensive tool that enhances productivity, facilitates collaboration, and ensures data is readily accessible from any device, anywhere.

In this final section, we will take a moment to reflect on the key takeaways from this guide and offer some final thoughts on why cloud storage, particularly Dropbox, plays such a vital role in the modern digital ecosystem.

The Growing Importance of Cloud Storage

Cloud storage has evolved significantly over the years. What once started as a simple tool for backing up files has grown into an essential service that powers much of the digital economy. Businesses, educational institutions, non-profits, and individuals now rely on cloud platforms for a variety of needs. Whether you're saving photos, documents, or complex databases, cloud storage provides a scalable solution for everyone.

One of the most significant benefits of cloud storage is its flexibility. Users can access their files from any internet-connected device, ensuring that work, personal data, and important projects are always within reach. This flexibility is essential in a world where remote work, freelance careers, and mobile lifestyles are becoming the norm.

Dropbox is at the forefront of this shift in digital storage, offering not just a place to store files but a complete platform for collaboration, file sharing, and synchronization. It allows users to store their files with the confidence that they are secure, accessible, and ready for collaboration with just a few clicks. As cloud storage continues to become a more essential part of everyday life, understanding its role and impact will only become more important.

Embracing Cloud Storage for Collaboration and Efficiency

One of the most powerful aspects of cloud storage is its ability to facilitate collaboration. Dropbox has integrated tools that enable real-time collaboration on documents, presentations, and spreadsheets, ensuring that teams can work together regardless of geographic location. Gone are the days of emailing files back and forth or dealing with version control issues. With Dropbox, multiple users can access and edit files simultaneously, eliminating the confusion of trying to figure out which version is the most recent.

For businesses, this has been revolutionary. Teams can now share files, communicate, and manage projects in a seamless workflow. Dropbox Paper, for instance, enables teams to brainstorm, plan, and work on content creation without the need for separate applications. It serves as an all-in-one workspace for teams to collaborate efficiently. When combined with other productivity tools and integrations—such as Google Workspace, Microsoft Office, and Slack—Dropbox becomes a central hub for managing and executing work projects in real-time.

For personal use, cloud storage allows individuals to organize and share files without worrying about losing important documents or files due to a broken hard drive or lost device. With Dropbox, files are always safe, secure, and available across devices. Whether it's a family photo album or a school project, the ability to access files from any device, anytime, brings unmatched convenience.

Cloud Storage and Security: Peace of Mind for Users

Security is one of the primary concerns for anyone using cloud storage, and Dropbox has made this a top priority. With a combination of encryption, two-factor authentication, and a strong privacy policy, Dropbox ensures that your files are protected from unauthorized access. Files stored in Dropbox are encrypted both during transit and at rest, which means that even if a hacker gains access to the data, they cannot read it without the proper encryption keys.

Dropbox's security measures go beyond just encrypting data. With features like file versioning and recovery, users can restore earlier versions of files, giving them peace of mind in case of accidental deletion or edits. Moreover, if you've shared files or folders with others, Dropbox allows you to manage access permissions, ensuring that only authorized individuals can view or edit files. This is particularly important for businesses that store sensitive data and need to maintain strict control over who has access to their documents.

As cloud storage becomes more widespread, security challenges will continue to evolve. However, platforms like Dropbox are committed to staying ahead of these challenges, offering users a combination of technological safeguards and user-friendly features to ensure that their files remain secure.

The Future of Cloud Storage

Looking to the future, cloud storage is only going to grow in importance. The expansion of the Internet of Things (IoT), artificial intelligence (AI), and machine learning (ML) will require vast amounts of data storage, processing, and sharing. As these technologies continue to advance, the role of cloud storage will become even more critical in managing, securing, and utilizing the data that powers these innovations.

Dropbox, along with other cloud storage services, will likely continue to evolve and expand its feature set to meet the needs of businesses and individuals in an increasingly connected world. From AI-powered file organization to smarter collaboration tools, the future of Dropbox and cloud storage as a whole looks bright. Expect more integrations with emerging technologies, deeper automation, and even better cross-platform functionality, which will make cloud storage even more seamless and accessible.

For individuals, the continued development of cloud storage services means that managing personal files and digital media will only get easier. As new features are introduced, Dropbox and other services will continue to refine their user experience, ensuring that anyone, regardless of their technical expertise, can easily store, share, and access their files without difficulty.

Embracing Cloud Storage for a Better Digital Future

As we conclude this book, it's essential to recognize that cloud storage is not just a convenience; it is a fundamental tool that is shaping the way we live, work, and interact with the world around us. Dropbox is one of the many platforms that exemplifies this shift, offering an intuitive, user-friendly experience that supports both personal and professional growth.

For businesses, cloud storage is no longer optional. It is a critical tool for maintaining productivity, fostering collaboration, and staying competitive in an increasingly digital world. For individuals, it provides peace of mind and a sense of security, knowing that files are always protected, organized, and accessible.

In the end, adopting cloud storage services like Dropbox is more than just a technological choice; it's a step toward embracing the future of digital storage and collaboration. As we continue to rely on digital tools for almost every aspect of our lives, understanding the power of cloud storage will be crucial. With Dropbox, users are equipped to manage, protect, and collaborate on their digital assets, ensuring that they stay ahead in an ever-changing world.

As cloud technology continues to evolve, the best is yet to come. By embracing the tools and features available today, you are preparing yourself for the digital challenges of tomorrow. Dropbox is ready to help you store, share, and collaborate more effectively than ever before.

Acknowledgments

I would like to take a moment to sincerely thank you, the reader, for purchasing **Cloud Storage Made Simple: Your Guide to Dropbox**. *Your decision to invest time in this book means a great deal to me, and I hope it has provided you with valuable insights into maximizing your use of Dropbox and cloud storage in general.*

In today's rapidly evolving digital landscape, it's crucial to stay informed and adaptable. By choosing to read this book, you are taking a step toward mastering one of the most powerful tools for organizing, securing, and sharing your digital world. I truly believe that by applying the strategies and tips within these pages, you'll be able to optimize your workflow and achieve greater efficiency in both personal and professional environments.

I am grateful for your support in bringing this project to life. Whether you're a beginner just starting to explore cloud storage or a seasoned professional looking to refine your skills, I hope you found this guide helpful and informative.

Thank you again for being a part of this journey. I wish you all the best in your continued exploration of Dropbox and the world of cloud storage. May your files remain organized, secure, and always within reach!

With sincere gratitude,